PRACTICAL
ENGLISH
WORKBOOK

PRACTICAL ENGLISH WORKBOOK

Fourth Edition

Floyd C. Watkins
EMORY UNIVERSITY

William B. Dillingham
EMORY UNIVERSITY

John T. Hiers
VALDOSTA STATE COLLEGE

HOUGHTON MIFFLIN COMPANY • BOSTON

DALLAS   GENEVA, ILL.   PALO ALTO   PRINCETON, N.J.

Cover: *Ocean Park Series No. 40.* 1971. Richard Diebenkorn, private collection.

Grateful acknowledgment is made to the following publishers and authors for permission to reprint from their works:

The American Heritage Dictionary of the English Language. Definition of *bureaucrat.* © 1981 by Houghton Mifflin Company. Reprinted by permission from *The American Heritage Dictionary of the English Language.*

William A. Henry, "Journalism Under Fire." Copyright 1983 Time Inc. All rights reserved. Reprinted by permission from *Time*.

Norman Myers, "By Saving Wild Species, We May Be Saving Ourselves." Originally published in the Nov./Dec. 1983 *TNC News.* Reprinted by permission of *The Nature Conservancy News*.

Francis Parkman, *The Oregon Trail.* Riverside Literature Series, edited with introduction and notes. Copyright © 1925 by Houghton Mifflin Company. Adapted by permission.

Francis Christensen, *Notes Toward a New Rhetoric: Six Essays for Teachers.* Copyright © 1967 by Francis Christensen. Reprinted by permission of Harper & Row Publishers, Inc.

ISBN: 0-395-49261-0

BCDEFGHIJ-M-9543210-89

CONTENTS

SENTENCE STRUCTURE   117

10   Coordination, Subordination, Completeness, Comparisons, and Consistency   118

11   Position of Modifiers, Separation of Elements, Parallelism, and Sentence Variety   141

PUNCTUATION   175

12   Commas   176

13   Unnecessary Commas   201

14   Semicolons, Colons, Dashes, Parentheses, and Brackets   207

15   Quotation Marks and End Punctuation   219

MECHANICS   225

16   Underlining for Italics   226

17   Spelling   233

22   Connotation, Figurative Language, Flowery Language, and Vocabulary   321

PARAGRAPHS   335

23   Identifying Paragraphs and Sentence Functions   336

24   Paragraph Development   357

25   Paragraph Transitions   365

PREFACE

The organization of the Fourth Edition of *Practical English Workbook* closely follows that of *Practical English Handbook*, Eighth Edition. For those students who require more practice with basic skills, this workbook is designed to reinforce the instruction of the handbook with parallel lessons, additional examples, and varied exercises. Beginning with parts of speech, the workbook also provides lessons on parts of sentences, sentence errors, punctuation, mechanics, diction and style, and paragraphs. The logical sequence of these lessons makes *Practical English Workbook* adaptable to other texts as well as to independent study and laboratory instruction for students at all levels.

For the Fourth Edition we have undertaken a thorough revision of PRACTICAL ENGLISH WORKBOOK. We have

- improved all instructional sections, giving more examples and more complete coverage of grammatical points.
- greatly expanded the section on writing effective paragraphs.
- added twenty-four new exercises (including end-of-unit review exercises and many paragraph-length editing activities). These additions give PRACTICAL ENGLISH WORKBOOK greater range and depth.
- revised all exercises.

As with the Third Edition, we have kept the style concise and readable, avoiding the extremes of colloquialism and rigid formality. This edition, as did its predecessor, stresses clarity and precision.

Like *Practical English Handbook*, this edition of *Practical English Workbook* follows a traditional approach to grammar, punctuation, and syntax. We believe that this method has proven itself over the years as the best means to call attention to writing problems and to improve the writing skills of students. This mainstream approach to grammar, punctuation, and syntax has dictated the workbook's methodology. We have worked toward stating the most useful rules in the simplest form possible and have stressed typical problems in both examples and exercises.

Throughout the text, emphasis is upon building writing skills and developing the student's understanding of the well-established practices governing the use of the English language.

We are deeply indebted to Professor Byron Brown of Valdosta State College for his aid and advice. We also wish to thank Richard Charnigo, Cuyahoga Community College, Ohio; Judith A. Deisler, St. Petersburg Junior College, Florida; Susanne Popper Edelman, Long Island University, New York; Karen N. Gleeman, Normandale Community College, Minnesota; C. Jeriel Howard, Northeastern Illinois University; Patricia Licklider, John Jay College of Criminal Justice, City University of New York; Judith A. Longo, Ocean County College, New Jersey; Kathy Routon, Sierra College, California; and Stephen F. Wozniak, Palomar College, California, for their thoughtful reading of the manuscript.

F. C. W.
W. B. D.
J. T. H.

PRACTICAL
ENGLISH
WORKBOOK

GRAMMAR

1 The Parts of Speech

There are eight parts of speech in the English language: nouns, pronouns, verbs, adjectives, adverbs, conjunctions, prepositions, and interjections.

NOUNS

Nouns are words that name. There are five kinds of nouns: proper nouns, common nouns, collective nouns, abstract nouns, and concrete nouns.

(a) **Proper nouns** name particular persons, places, or things *(Thomas Edison, Chicago, Kleenex)*.

   Commodore Perry sailed to *Japan* on the U.S.S. *Mississippi*.

(b) **Common nouns** name one or more of a class or group *(doctor, pilots, artists)*.

   Roger placed a *vase* of freshly cut *flowers* on the *table*.

(c) **Collective nouns** name a whole group, though they are singular in form *(senate, jury, clergy)*.

   Our *committee* will consider the proposal at its next meeting.

(d) **Abstract nouns** name concepts, beliefs, or qualities *(truth, energy, humor)*.

   Freedom implies *responsibility*.

(e) **Concrete nouns** name things experienced through the senses *(fire, coffee, roses)*.

   Hundreds of *acorns* littered the *ground* under the large *oak*.

PRONOUNS

There are seven kinds of pronouns. Most pronouns are used in place of nouns, although indefinite pronouns do not refer to any particular noun.

(a) **Demonstrative pronouns** summarize in one word the content of a statement that has already been made. They can be singular *(this, that)* or plural *(these, those)*.

Fruit, bran, whole wheat—*these* are common sources of healthful fiber.

(b) **Indefinite pronouns** do not indicate a particular person or thing. They are usually singular. The most common indefinite pronouns are *any, anybody, anyone, everybody, everyone, neither, none, one,* and *some.*

Neither of her roommates shares her love of progressive jazz.

(c) **Intensive pronouns** end in *-self* or *-selves* (*herself, themselves*). An intensive pronoun emphasizes a word that precedes it in the sentence.

She *herself* was surprised at her quick success.
The committee *itself* was confused.

(d) **Interrogative pronouns** (*what, which, who, whom, whose, whoever, whomever*) are used in questions.

Who posted that notice on the bulletin board?
What was the final score?

(e) **Personal pronouns** usually refer to a person or a group of people, but may refer to an object or objects. They have many forms, depending on their grammatical function.

Ask *her* whether *she* has called *him* yet.
After *he* waxed *his* car, *he* parked *it* in the garage.

	SINGULAR	PLURAL
First person	I, me, mine	we, us, ours
Second person	you, yours	you, yours
Third person	he, she, it, him, her, his, hers, its	they, them, theirs

(f) **Reflexive pronouns** end in *-self* or *-selves* and indicate that the subject acts upon itself.

He caught *himself* making the same mistake twice.
The broken flywheel caused the machine to destroy *itself.*

(g) **Relative pronouns** (*who, whom, whoever, whomever, whichever, whose, that, what, which*) are used to introduce dependent adjective and noun clauses.

You can eat the pie *that is in the refrigerator.* (adjective clause modifying *pie,* introduced by the relative pronoun *that*)
The workers *who had finished* began to leave. (noun clause)

3

VERBS

Verbs assert an action or express a condition.

> The bus *screeched* to a stop. (verb showing *action*)
> The capital of Missouri *is* Jefferson City. (verb showing *condition*)

Verbs that show *condition* are called **linking verbs.** The most common linking verbs are forms of the verb *to be (is, are, was, were).* Other linking verbs are *seem, become, look, appear, feel, sound, smell,* and *taste.*

> The music *is* discordant, yet interesting.

Main verbs may have **auxiliary verbs,** or helpers, such as *are, have, may, will.*

> Renovation of the old house *may* take up to a year.

ADJECTIVES

Adjectives are descriptive words that modify nouns or pronouns. The **definite article** *the* and the **indefinite articles** *a* and *an* are also classified as adjectives.

> The *brilliant* sunset left us breathless.

Predicate adjectives follow linking verbs and modify the subject of the sentence.

> The article is *informative.*
> The car looks *new.*

Some **possessive adjectives** have forms that are similar to possessive pronouns: *my, your, her, his, its, their.* These adjectives refer to specific nouns just as pronouns do, but function as adjectives. *Your, our,* and *their* end with *s* in the pronoun form.

> *Your* dinner is ready.

Demonstrative adjectives and demonstrative pronouns have the same forms: *this, that, these, those.* (See demonstrative pronouns, p. 2.)

> *This* comment is helpful. (*This* modifies *comment.*)
> *This* is a helpful comment. (*This* is used here as a demonstrative pronoun.)

Indefinite adjectives resemble indefinite pronouns: *some, many, most, every.*

Every employee received a bonus. (*Every* modifies *employee*.)

Everyone left. (*Everyone* is an indefinite pronoun.)

ADVERBS

Adverbs describe, qualify, or limit verbs (and verbals), adjectives, and other adverbs.

The cashier laughed *uproariously*. (adverb—modifies a verb)

Be sure to read the instructions *carefully*. (adverb—modifies the verbal *to read*)

The train was *very* late. (adverb—modifies the adjective *late*)

We shall be through *very* soon. (adverb—modifies another adverb, *soon*)

Many adverbs are formed by adding *-ly* to adjectives; others express place or time: *soon, later, always, forever, there, out.*

Bring the newspaper *inside*. (*Inside* expresses place.)

Bring me the newspaper *now*. (*Now* expresses time.)

CONJUNCTIONS

Conjunctions connect words, phrases, and clauses. Conjunctive adverbs — *therefore, however, furthermore, moreover* — connect clauses and phrases.

Hang gliding has few adherents; most of them, *however*, are quite devoted to the sport.

Coordinating conjunctions — *and, but, or, nor, for, yet, so* — connect sentence elements that are of equal rank.

Music boxes *and* bric-a-brac lined the shelves of the gift shop. (conjunction joining two nouns)

We called the apartment manager, *but* she was not at home. (conjunction joining two independent clauses)

Subordinating conjunctions introduce a dependent clause in a sentence—that is, one that cannot stand alone as a sentence. Some common subordinating conjunctions are *although, because, if, since, unless*, and *when*.

When we finished the test. (dependent element, not a sentence)

When we finished the test, we turned in our papers. (dependent element joined to independent clause to form a complete sentence)

We were tired *because we had studied all night*. (dependent element joined to independent clause to form a complete sentence)

PREPOSITIONS

Prepositions are connective words that join nouns or pronouns to other words in a sentence to form a unit (called a **prepositional phrase**). Prepositional phrases function as either adjectives or adverbs. Some prepositions are *above, at, before, by, from, in, into, of, over, through, up,* and *with*. Some groups of words (*according to, in spite of, along with*) may also function as prepositions.

> The jet flew *through the clouds*. (*Through the clouds* is a prepositional phrase used as an adverb to modify the verb *flew*.)
>
> The woman *in the car* is my mother. (*In the car* is a prepositional phrase used as an adjective to modify the noun *woman*.)

Some words that resemble prepositions function as adverbs:

> Go out. (*out* used as adverb)
>
> Go out the door. (*out* used as preposition)

Some words, such as *before* and *after*, may function as prepositions or subordinating conjunctions.

INTERJECTIONS

Interjections are words that express surprise or strong emotions. They may stand alone or be part of a sentence. Interjections usually are avoided in formal writing.

> *Wow!*
>
> *Well*, you should have been more careful.

1.1 Nouns

■ *Underline the words used as nouns in the following sentences.*

EXAMPLES
Educational <u>television</u> needs private <u>donations</u>.
<u>Marshall</u>'s coin <u>collection</u> is quite valuable.
<u>Ronald Reagan</u> succeeded <u>Jimmy Carter</u> as <u>President</u>.

1. Community historical societies plan the restoration of old buildings.

2. Several archaeological excavations clarify the Biblical accounts of the era of Solomon.

3. Road atlases provide convenient guides for cross-country travelers.

4. Winter rains replenish depleted water tables.

5. Early in the century two hundred button-making factories in the United States almost depleted the supply of fresh-water mussels.

6. Some veterinarians have found acupuncture to be of value in the treatment of animals.

7. The Galapagos Islands, volcanic in origin and isolated in the Pacific Ocean, offer many biological wonders.

8. Selenium in small doses is a necessary part of the human diet.

9. Cuna Indians inhabit the eastern shore of Panama.

10. Generations of writers and artists have been inspired by the mythology of ancient Greece and Rome.

1.2 Pronouns

■ *Underline the pronouns in the following sentences.*

EXAMPLES

<u>She</u> <u>herself</u> intends to represent the clients. (personal, intensive pronouns)

<u>Those</u> students <u>who</u> want to view the art exhibit will find <u>it</u> in Roswell Hall, <u>which</u> is next to the library. (demonstrative, relative, personal, relative pronouns)

Meg wants <u>everyone</u> to try her new recipe. (indefinite pronoun)

1. Nobody spoke against the proposal, but each of us had reasons to object to it.

2. Neither of the restaurants offered authentic Vietnamese cuisine to its customers.

3. You will almost always find Edie playing a video game because she enjoys the challenge.

4. All of the silver needs polishing before we set the table.

5. Fortunately, none of the crop was ruined by the ice storm.

6. Signaling to those who steadied her ladder, the firefighter began her long descent.

7. Harry and his wife promised themselves that they would do their holiday shopping earlier next year.

8. Resisting discouragement, the fisherman stretched himself and waited for his luck to change.

9. The problem itself was easy to understand, but the solution required working through several steps.

10. Whatever they did to follow their budget, they rarely managed to stay within it.

1.3 Verbs

■ *Underline the verbs in the following sentences.*

EXAMPLES

Technology <u>raises</u> hope for greater crop yields. (action verb)

Marketing through cable television <u>is</u> often effective. (linking verb showing condition)

Economists <u>will remain</u> optimistic about the recovery. (auxiliary verb and linking verb showing condition)

1. Coconut palms can reach a height of one hundred feet.

2. Many athletes fail, not because they are out of condition but because they develop mental blocks.

3. Many collectors especially value Dresden china.

4. The children went to the doctor and had their annual physical examinations.

5. A congressional committee on housing will be in the Midwest to discuss the special needs of local communities.

6. People once believed that toothaches were a sign that some god was angry.

7. U. S. Grant's early victories won him the attention of the public and contributed to his rapid promotion.

8. The lighting in the restaurant was so dim that the diners could hardly read the menu.

9. The conveniences that most enjoy in their lives today would have required the labor of at least eighty servants a century ago.

10. Did the electrician follow your directions, or did he find the house by himself?

1.4 Adjectives

■ *Underline the words used as adjectives in the following sentences. Remember that* articles (a, an, the) *are also classified as adjectives.*

EXAMPLES
The fragile crystal decanter tottered precariously on the uneven tabletop.
Many new word processing programs are extremely versatile. (predicate adjective following the linking verb *are*)

1. The puzzled historian stared at the faded painting of the royal couple.

2. At the circus the children laughed and clapped as fifteen clowns emerged from the small car.

3. In 1904 the famous Geronimo rode in the inaugural parade of Theodore Roosevelt.

4. Some winter campers use small propane heaters to combat cold weather.

5. Tremendous ovations that follow performances please young performers.

6. Oceanographic teams study the fragile sea life along the coral reefs near Key West, Florida.

7. The fascinated children surrounded the sad-eyed clown and his lively monkey.

8. The late movie was a film made in the 1930s.

9. Coral reefs are as dangerous as they are interesting.

10. Gauguin's paintings frequently combine brilliant colors and distorted landscapes.

1.5 Adverbs

■ *Underline the words used as adverbs in the following sentences.*

EXAMPLES

<u>More</u> modest increases in prices <u>usually</u> are expected. (adverb modifying an adjective and a verb)

The news is <u>almost completely</u> certain to arouse controversy. (adverb modifying another adverb and adverb modifying an adjective)

1. The agile gymnast fearlessly mounted the balance beam.

2. The office seldom closes before five o'clock.

3. Caterpillars move slowly but purposefully up the stems of plants.

4. The careful manager always ordered his inventory well in advance.

5. Because surgeons work cautiously with lasers, some procedures take longer than usual.

6. Samuel Taylor Coleridge's conversation was usually stimulating and sometimes profound.

7. While carefully examining the walls of the ancient building, the archaeologist suddenly discovered a small cache of coins that easily were over two thousand years old.

8. The flowers were covered partially by late spring frost that quickly melted when the sun rose.

9. As the morning fog quietly rolled in over the city, the traffic gradually slowed.

10. Candidates who speak forcefully rather than deliberately often are more effective with voters.

1.6 Conjunctions, Prepositions, and Interjections

■ *Underline prepositions in the following sentences once, conjunctions twice, and interjections three times.*

EXAMPLES

"<u><u><u>Oh</u></u></u>," said the novelist, "I found the first <u><u>and</u></u> last chapters <u>of</u> the novel were the most difficult to write." (interjection, coordinating conjunction, preposition)

<u><u>Although</u></u> the winds were strong, the boaters began the race <u>for</u> the gold cup. (subordinating conjunction, preposition)

1. Thousands of Mardi Gras revelers filled the streets and avenues with color and song.

2. When mature, koalas may weigh thirty pounds, but at birth they weigh only one fifth of an ounce.

3. Birds build nests in chimneys, and these must be removed before winter.

4. Often researchers find themselves on the brink of discoveries far more important than they originally imagined.

5. Experimental results should be checked carefully, for later findings may depend on them.

6. "Well, if this letter does not work," the disgruntled consumer said, "I shall write again."

7. The speaker's points were provocative; however, his delivery was wooden.

8. "No!" responded the officer. "I do not accept your answer."

9. The rain came early in the morning, so the yard work was postponed.

10. People do not seem to realize the need to conserve energy, nor do they comprehend the consequences if they do not.

1.7 Same Word; Several Functions

■ *Many words can function as several parts of speech. Compose very brief sentences with the following words, illustrating the parts of speech in parentheses. If necessary, check a dictionary.*

EXAMPLES

right (noun) *The jury had to decide what was right in the complex case.*

right (adjective) *The right side of the highway was beautiful in its spring colors.*

right (adverb) *The new attorney rose right to the top of his profession.*

1. like (preposition) _____

_____

_____

(adjective) _____

_____

_____

(verb) _____

_____

_____

2. water (noun) _____

_____

_____

(verb) _____

_____

_____

(adjective) _____

_____

3. well (noun) _____

_____

_____

(interjection) _____

_____

_____

(adverb) _____

_____

_____

4. light (noun) _____

_____

_____

(adjective) _____

_____

_____

(verb) _____

_____

_____

5. fine (adjective) _____

_____

_____

(noun) _____

_____

(verb) _____

_____

6. house (noun) _____

_____

(adjective) _____

_____

(verb) _____

_____

7. total (noun) _____

_____

(adjective) _____

_____

(verb) _____

_____

8. sound (noun) _____

_____

(adjective) _____

_____

_____

(verb) _____

_____

_____

9. stock (noun) _____

_____

_____

(verb) _____

_____

_____

(adjective) _____

_____

_____

10. down (noun) _____

_____

_____

(verb) _____

_____

_____

(preposition) _____

_____

_____

1.8 Parts of Speech: Review

■ *Identify the part of speech of the italicized words.*

    Doctors have *many ways* to help the millions of Americans *who suffer* from back pain. Many of *these* people would be *almost completely* paralyzed if not for modern treatments. Patients *with* acute pain *respond* well to a *combination* of medication and physical therapy, including *a* regime of massage *and* ultrasound. People with *less* serious back problems find mild exercise under *controlled* conditions to be helpful. Experts *especially* recommend whirlpool baths; the *warm* water apparently *helps their* patients' muscles relax.

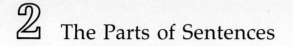

2 The Parts of Sentences

SUBJECTS AND PREDICATES

A sentence has a complete meaning and can stand on its own. Its essential parts are its subject and predicate.

The **subject** does something, has something done to it, or is described.

> The *woman* is reading. (subject acting)
> *Books* are read. (subject acted upon)
> *Books* are interesting. (subject described)

In sentences that command, a subject may be understood.

> Go to the den. (*You* is the understood subject.)

The **predicate** says something about the subject.

> The woman *is reading.*
> Books *are sources of information.*
> Books *are interesting.*

The **simple subject** usually consists of one word. The **complete subject** consists of all the words that function together as the subject.

> The *house* is dark. (simple subject)
> *The old house* is dark. (complete subject)

When similar units of a sentence are linked together and function together, they are termed **compound.**

> *The automobile* and *the truck* stopped. (compound subject)

The verb in a sentence is called the **simple predicate.** The simple predicate, its modifiers, and any complements are called the **complete predicate.**

> Harry *finished* his work. (simple predicate)
> Harry *finished his work.* (complete predicate)
> She *researched* the topic and *wrote* the paper. (compound predicate)

COMPLEMENTS

Complements complete the meaning of the sentence. They are predicate adjectives, predicate nominatives, direct objects, and indirect objects.

Predicate adjectives and predicate nominatives are also called **subjective complements.**

Predicate adjectives follow linking verbs and describe the subject.

> Her voice is *beautiful.* (predicate adjective describing *voice*)
>
> Some problems seem *insoluble.* (predicate adjective after linking verb)

Predicate nominatives are nouns that follow linking verbs and rename the subject.

> Tonight's lecturer is an *expert* on tax law. (predicate nominative renaming *lecturer*)

Direct objects receive the action of a transitive verb.

> We played *Scrabble.* (direct object telling what was played)

Indirect objects receive the action of the verb indirectly. When the preposition *to* or *for* is understood, the word is an indirect object. A sentence with an indirect object must also have a direct object.

> Sheila gave *me* a present. (indirect object telling *to whom* the present was given)

Objective complements accompany direct objects. They may modify the object or be synonymous with it.

> The new owner painted his house *red.* (adjective modifying the direct object *house*)

PHRASES

A **phrase** is a group of words that does not have both a subject and a predicate.

A **noun phrase** consists of a noun and its modifiers.

> *A graceful old elm tree* towered over the house.

An **appositive phrase** renames a noun.

> George, *our new office manager,* met with his staff this morning.

A **verb phrase** consists of the main verb and its helping verbs.

> The house *is being painted.*

Prepositional phrases function as adjectives or adverbs.

The door *to the closet* is open. (adjectival phrase modifying *door*)

The rain fell *in the park.* (adverbial phrase modifying *fell*)

VERBALS AND VERBAL PHRASES

A **verbal** is formed from a verb. Three kinds of verbals are gerunds, participles, and infinitives.

Gerunds

A **gerund** always ends in *-ing* and functions as a noun.

> *Hiking the Appalachian Trail* is fun. (gerund phrase as subject)
>
> Before *hiking the Appalachian Trail,* a person needs to make careful preparations. (gerund phrase as the object of the preposition *before*)

Participles

Participles usually end in *-ing, -ed, -d, -t,* or *-n.* They function as adjectives.

> *Determined* to complete the report on time, Bill renewed his efforts. (modifies *Bill*)
>
> *Encouraging to the board of directors,* the report predicted record profits. (modifies *report; encouraging to the board of directors* is the complete participial phrase)

Infinitives

Infinitives usually begin with *to,* which is followed by a verb. They function as nouns, adjectives, or adverbs.

> *To show the new student around our school* took time. (infinitive phrase as subject)
>
> Camera cases *to be carried on the trip* must be waterproof. (infinitive phrase as adjective)
>
> *To be certain of lodging,* one should make reservations. (infinitive phrase as adverb)
>
> The children helped their father *plant the garden.* (infinitive phrase without *to*)

CLAUSES

Clauses are groups of words with subjects and predicates. Clauses are either independent or dependent (sometimes called *subordinate).*

An **independent clause** can stand alone as a complete sentence. Two or more independent clauses may be linked (1) by coordinating conjunctions *(and, but, or, nor, for, so, yet)* and a comma, (2) by a semicolon, or (3) by a semicolon and a **conjunctive adverb** (such as *however, therefore, moreover, nevertheless, otherwise*).

> The circus is over, *and* the workers are cleaning the grounds. (two independent clauses connected by a comma and a coordinating conjunction)
>
> The river was crowded with barges; each one of them was piled high with coal from the mines of Kentucky and West Virginia. (two independent clauses joined by a semicolon)
>
> Low clouds obscured much of the mountain; *however,* the snow-covered peak sparkled in the bright sunlight. (two independent clauses joined by a semicolon and a conjunctive adverb)

A **dependent** or **subordinate clause** can function as a noun, an adjective, or an adverb.

> *Who the next chairman will be* remains a secret. (noun clause as subject)
>
> The salesman *who opened the most new accounts* won a trip to the Bahamas. (adjective clause modifying *salesman*)
>
> *When the master of ceremonies announced the winner,* the audience applauded enthusiastically. (adverb clause modifying *applauded*)

NAME _____

DATE _____ SCORE _____

2.1 The Parts of Sentences

■ *Underline the simple or compound subjects once and the simple or compound predicates twice. Identify complements with the abbreviations **p.a.** (predicate adjective), **p.n.** (predicate nominative), **d.o.** (direct object), **i.o.** (indirect object), and **o.c.** (objective complement) above the appropriate words.*

EXAMPLES

d.o.
Silicon chips have revolutionized the electronics industry.

i.o.   *d.o.*
Geologists gave investors the preliminary analysis of several oil wells.

1. The solution to the dilemma came only after long study.

2. Echoes of the song's refrain haunted the reveler's memory.

3. Contrast and repetition are the two main ingredients in musical form.

4. Stockbrokers sometimes give their clients advice about a variety of investments.

5. Brahms wrote four symphonies.

6. Interesting floral arrangements contain a profusion of blossoms.

7. Spanish treasure ships laden with gold, silver, and gems are still being discovered in the Caribbean.

8. At airshows stunt pilots put their planes into steep power stalls and then slip into dives.

9. Neither the boy nor his dog seemed willing for the parade to end.

10. The blackberry is edible, and it is used often in pastries.

2.2 The Parts of Sentences

■ *Underline the simple or compound subjects once and the simple or compound predicates twice. Identify complements with the abbreviations **p.a.** (predicate adjective), **p.n.** (predicate nominative), **d.o.** (direct object), and **i.o.** (indirect object) above the appropriate words.*

EXAMPLES

p.a.

Those <u>slides</u> of the ancient Incan ruins <u><u>were</u></u> fascinating.

p.n.

<u>She</u> <u><u>became</u></u> president of the holding company last week.

1. At family reunions, grandparents often regale their grandchildren with outrageous stories about their youth.

2. The Soviet Union is the world's largest producer of wheat.

3. Many experienced distance runners have resting heartrates of less than fifty beats a minute.

4. Hungarian composer Franz Liszt was instrumental in shaping the career of Johannes Brahms.

5. Latin America was settled primarily by Europeans from Spain and Portugal.

6. Arthur Wynne devised the first crossword puzzle in 1913 for the *New York World.*

7. The International Balloon Fiesta takes place each year in Albuquerque, New Mexico.

8. Even microcomputers can store large amounts of information in their random-access memories.

9. Salaries for federal employees are highest in Alaska.

10. One notices immediately the differences between the two cultures, especially in their art.

2.3 Phrases

■ *On the blank lines, indicate whether the italicized phrase is used as noun, modifier, verbal, or verb, and indicate its function in the sentence.*

EXAMPLES

Using credit cards is a way *of life* for modern Americans.

modifier—prepositional phrase modifying noun way

The scientists, *concerned about the potential hazards,* wanted the latest research findings made public.

modifier—participial phrase modifying noun scientists

Keeping their bodies in good condition is a primary concern of many young Americans.

noun—gerund phrase as subject of is

1. Alchemists *of the Middle Ages* tried to transform lead into gold.

   _____

2. The children raced to the corner *to catch their bus.*

   _____

3. *Talking with an insurance agent* makes people realize that they need additional coverage for their home.

   _____

4. *To date fossil remains* requires several hours of careful laboratory work.

   _____

5. Blue whales, the world's largest mammals, are still threatened *by extinction.*

   _____

6. The chinook winds whip down the eastern slopes of the Rocky Mountains and sweep *across the vast prairies*.

   _____

7. Construction *of the new civic center and parkway* revived the sagging economy of downtown businesses.

   _____

8. On each side of the highway were hundreds of billboards *advertising everything* from modern motels to roadside stands that sell fresh fruit and bedspreads.

   _____

9. The corporate merger *will have been planned* far in advance of the public announcement.

   _____

10. *The tour bus* stopped in Savannah so that the tourists could visit the beautiful old homes that date back to the last part of the eighteenth century.

    _____

2.4 Phrases

■ *Write sentences containing the following words in the prescribed phrases.*

EXAMPLE
continue; verb phrase

Tardiness and absenteeism are continuing to pose serious problems for many American businesses.

1. *surprised;* participial phrase modifying the subject and placed before the verb

   _____

   _____

   _____

2. *to hear;* infinitive phrase used as an object

   _____

   _____

   _____

3. *giving;* gerund phrase used as an object of a preposition

   _____

   _____

   _____

4. *between;* prepositional phrase

   _____

   _____

   _____

5. *from;* prepositional phrase

   _____

6. *restored*; verb phrase

7. *becoming*; verb phrase

8. *except*; prepositional phrase

9. *speech*; noun phrase

10. *illuminate*; verb phrase

11. *featured*; participial phrase

36

12. *refuge;* noun phrase

_____

_____

_____

13. *treasure;* verb phrase

_____

_____

_____

14. *changing;* gerund phrase as object of preposition

_____

_____

_____

15. *to divide;* infinitive phrase

_____

_____

_____

16. *trust;* verb phrase

_____

_____

_____

17. *below;* prepositional phrase

_____

_____

_____

18. *coat;* noun phrase

_____

_____

_____

19. *participate*; verb phrase

_____

_____

_____

20. *determination*; noun phrase

_____

_____

_____

2.5 Verbal Phrases

■ *Underline verbal phrases in the following sentences. Identify the verbal phrase as participial, infinitive, or gerund, its part of speech, and its function.*

EXAMPLES

Stretching for several blocks, the traffic jam tested the drivers' patience.

participial phrase used as adjective to modify traffic jam

To visit the Baseball Hall of Fame is every young boy's dream.

infinitive phrase (noun) used as subject of verb is

1. Delighted by the clown's playful antics, the toddler shrieked gleefully and stomped her feet.

   _____

2. To annoy his opponent, the chess master gently tapped his fingers.

   _____

3. Ardent fans try to move closer to the front of the auditorium.

   _____

4. Constructed in 1885, the old house had a special charm about it.

   _____

5. Scientists have been able to find links between left-handedness and a number of diseases.

   _____

6. Trained to hunt small burrowing animals, the dachshund did not originate in Germany but in Egypt.

   _____

7. Exercising properly and eating well are essential for good health.

   _____

8. Focusing on the track before her, the sprinter awaited the sound of the starting pistol.

_____

9. The tourists wanted to revisit the Arch of Triumph and the Eiffel Tower before they left Paris.

_____

10. Founded in 1933, Black Mountain College lasted only twenty-three years.

_____

11. Marvin wanted to move his library into the garage.

_____

12. The defense attorney asked to review the evidence presented during the day's testimony.

_____

13. Using ultrasonic techniques, doctors can detect possible birth defects.

_____

14. One purpose of the National Endowment for the Humanities is to foster an awareness of our cultural inheritance.

_____

15. Peruvian Indians may support their families by weaving colorful ponchos.

_____

16. Shrimp fishermen do not support further draining of marshes.

_____

17. A major goal of psychology is learning how emotions influence behavior.

_____

18. Archaeologists, working under strenuous conditions in the Arctic, discovered toy dolls over five hundred years old.

_____

19. To enjoy television one needs a comfortable couch and a variety of snacks.

_____

20. The employees to be selected for awards must excel in sales.

_____

2.6 Clauses

■ *Write whether the dependent clauses are used as nouns, adjectives, or adverbs. Remember that dependent clauses can be parts of independent clauses.*

EXAMPLES

Although dieting is common, it is difficult. *adverb*

What the speaker said could not be heard. (dependent clause used as subject of independent clause) *noun*

The compact car *that establishes a reputation for quality* will always have a good market. *adjective*

1. *Whoever needs help understanding the instructions* should call the toll-free number provided on the enclosed card. _____

2. *While Samuel Johnson compiled his famous dictionary,* he employed the services of four assistants. _____

3. Ice cream, *which was commercially made as early as 1786,* was first sold in New York. _____

4. *Although the porpoise is a graceful animal,* its name is derived from two Latin words meaning "pig fish." _____

5. Many plays are so bad that theatergoers leave *after the first act ends.* _____

6. All of the young dogs *that were trained as guides* had been raised as family pets. _____

7. The foul weather *that had been expected for a week* finally arrived. _____

8. Mercenary fans will support *whichever team is winning.* _____

9. *Since we moved to town,* five new families have moved into our neighborhood. _____

10. *When the young reporter arrived,* she interviewed several celebrities. _____

11. *Whoever decides to run for president* must file a

financial statement for the Federal Election Commission.

12. Parents *who store poisonous chemicals in locked cabinets* are protecting their children's lives.

13. *When the use of ostrich feathers in fashions became popular a century ago,* many ranchers in the Southwest raised ostriches.

14. *What Samuel Taylor Coleridge meant in his poem "Kubla Khan"* is still a matter of debate.

15. *Although the football team was inexperienced,* it won the state championship.

16. *After the furniture store was renovated,* the owner held a gigantic sale.

17. Preferred stocks are marketed to *whoever is willing to pay a premium for less risk.*

18. Travelers' checks are honored at any bank *that sells them.*

19. The crowd was refused admission to the rally *because the auditorium was filled.*

20. *How the mayor plans to raise revenues* concerns the local business community.

2.7 Clauses

■ *Write sentences using the following coordinating or subordinating conjunctions or conjunctive adverbs to introduce or to connect clauses.*

EXAMPLES
if; to introduce a dependent clause

If the snow is not melted by 10:00 tomorrow, we will have to postpone the exhibit.

and; to connect two main clauses

The yellow fruit of the palm tree is tasty, and according to some scientists, it is also nutritious.

furthermore; to connect two main clauses

Anita neglected to take careful notes on her reading; furthermore, she did not make a careful bibliographic citation.

1. *while;* to introduce a dependent clause

_____

_____

2. *or;* to connect two main clauses

_____

_____

3. *yet;* to connect two main clauses

_____

_____

4. *where;* to introduce a dependent clause

_____

_____

5. *consequently;* to connect two main clauses

_____

_____

6. *nevertheless;* to connect two main clauses

_____

_____

7. *whoever;* to introduce a dependent clause

_____

_____

8. *although;* to introduce a dependent clause

_____

_____

9. *as;* to introduce a dependent clause

_____

_____

10. *unless;* to introduce a dependent clause

_____

_____

2.8 Phrases and Clauses

■ *Identify the type of each italicized phrase and clause.*

There are many theories about the fate of dinosaurs, (1) *the largest animals ever to walk the earth.* After (2) *existing for thousands of years,* (3) *these magnificent reptiles* suddenly disappeared (4) *without a trace.* Some archaeologists (5) *who have also studied astronomy* believe that a giant meteor hit the earth, stirring clouds of dust which blocked the sunlight, causing plants and then dinosaurs to die. (6) *Other scientists see another possible cause.* They believe that a major volcanic eruption, (7) *with a single massive blast,* could have produced enough ash to block the sun for years. (8) *Basing their opinions on data derived from space exploration and from recent volcanic activity on the earth,* many scientists believe that the dinosaurs disappeared so quickly that their fate had to be the result of a single catastrophe. (9) *To learn more,* these scientists (10) *are continuing* their collaborative efforts.

1. _____

2. _____

3. _____

4. _____

5. _____

6. _____

7. _____

8. _____

9. _____

10. _____

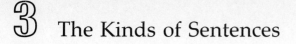 The Kinds of Sentences

There are four kinds of sentences: simple, compound, complex, and compound-complex.

A **simple sentence** has one independent clause.

> The antismoking lobby is becoming increasingly powerful. (one subject, one predicate)
>
> Many airlines as well as other businesses have imposed and enforced strict antismoking regulations. (compound subject, compound predicate)

A **compound sentence** contains two or more independent clauses joined by a coordinating conjunction or a semicolon.

> The new art show at the museum opened today, and the crowd was immense. (two independent clauses joined by *and*)
>
> The new art show at the museum opened today; the crowd was immense. (two independent clauses joined by a semicolon)

A **complex sentence** consists of one independent clause and one or more dependent clauses.

> After the sudden thunderstorm ended, the streets were filled with water. (dependent clause and independent clause)

A **compound-complex sentence** is a compound sentence with one or more dependent clauses.

> After the sudden thunderstorm ended, the streets were filled with water, and traffic was halted for nearly two hours. (dependent clause, independent clause, independent clause)

3.1 Kinds of Sentences

■ *Identify each of the following sentences as simple (s), compound (cd), complex (cx), or compound-complex (cd/cx).*

EXAMPLES

S   Everyone visiting Los Angeles should visit Disneyland.

cd   We ordered a pepperoni pizza, but the restaurant delivered one topped with anchovies and black olives.

cx   Nurseries that wholesale Christmas trees increase their off-season income.

cd/cx   Small pickup trucks, which are now popular in urban areas, are practical for the small business, and they outsell many larger models.

_____ 1. In 1847 Theobald Boehm designed the modern flute.

_____ 2. The beautiful arias and stirring choruses of Handel's *Messiah* make this oratorio a perennial favorite during the Christmas season.

_____ 3. The woman is a highly regarded critic, historian, and commentator, and she is also a faculty member at the university.

_____ 4. Moving south through Vermont, New Hampshire, Massachusetts, and Connecticut, the Connecticut River reaches the Atlantic Ocean.

_____ 5. D. W. Griffith directed over four hundred one-reel films between 1908 and 1913.

_____ 6. The beauty of writing lies not in how many words we know, but in the way we choose the words we use and how we organize them.

_____ 7. An object very similar to the modern bicycle is depicted in the wall art of ancient Egypt.

_____ 8. Although Maine has five letters in its name, it has only one syllable, two fewer than either Ohio or Iowa, which have only four letters each.

_____ 9. The water in the salt marshes along the southern Atlantic coast is replenished by the rising ocean tide.

_____ 10. Fallen trees, which may be hidden under the surface of the river, can cause extensive damage to fiberglass canoes, and there may be little white water to warn a canoeist of the danger.

3.2 Kinds of Sentences

■ *Write a brief paragraph on a topic of your choice. Use at least one simple sentence, one compound sentence, one complex sentence, and one compound-complex sentence. Label each kind of sentence in the margin.*

_____

_____

_____

_____

_____

_____

_____

_____

_____

_____

SENTENCE
ERRORS

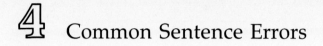

4 Common Sentence Errors

SENTENCE FRAGMENTS

Sentence fragments are incomplete sentences and usually consist of dependent clauses, phrases, or any other word group that does not make a complete thought. Fragments should be corrected by making the sentence complete.

NOT

> We looked for seats near the fifty-yard line. (complete sentence)
>
> So that we could see the football game better. (fragment: subordinate clause)

BUT

> We looked for seats near the fifty-yard line so that we could see the football game better.

COMMA SPLICES AND FUSED SENTENCES

A **comma splice** (or **comma fault**) occurs when two independent clauses are joined by a comma but have no coordinating conjunction (*and, or, nor, but, for, yet, so*).

NOT

> The movie was very exciting, we discussed it as we drove home.

BUT

> The movie was very exciting, *and* we discussed it as we drove home.

OR

> The movie was very exciting; we discussed it as we drove home.

A **fused sentence** (or **run-on**) occurs when two independent clauses have neither punctuation nor a conjunction between them.

NOT

> The driver did not see the icy spot on the road he was blinded by the sun's glare.

BUT

> The driver did not see the icy spot on the road; he was blinded by the sun's glare.

Comma splices and fused sentences can be corrected by writing two sentences, by using either a semicolon or a comma and a conjunction, or by making one of the sentences into a dependent clause.

> The driver did not see the icy spot on the road. He was blinded by the sun's glare. (two sentences)

The driver did not see the icy spot on the road; he was blinded by the sun's glare. (semicolon)

The driver did not see the icy spot on the road because he was blinded by the sun's glare. (dependent clause)

4.1 Sentence Fragments

■ *In the blanks at the right identify the following as complete sentences or as fragments.*

EXAMPLES
We love to eat at Tony's.   *sentence*
Because the atmosphere is relaxed there.   *fragment*
Snowdrifts are deep.   *sentence*
And the snow continues to fall.   *sentence*

1. Absorbed by the murder mystery's intriguing plot.   _____

   I read late into the night.   _____

2. After the dinner dance.   _____

   The band members packed their instruments.   _____

3. Beginning as a commercial artist and cartoonist in Kansas City.   _____

   Walt Disney moved to Hollywood in 1923.   _____

4. Spring flowers covered the field.   _____

   Almost dancing in the breeze.   _____

5. *Arsenic and Old Lace* was released in 1944.   _____

   Frank Capra directed this film.   _____

6. The rear tires being flat.   _____

   We called a garage.   _____

7. Quoting a famous American statesman.   _____

   The candidate then referred to his own plans.   _____

8. The type was too small.   _____

   The ink was blurred.   _____

9. To see the parade. _____

   The bands and the floats. _____

10. Being quiet people. _____

    Rarely object to anything. _____

4.2 Sentence Fragments

■ *Correct the following sentence fragments by joining them to the complete sentences.*

EXAMPLES

After driving all night and part of the morning. We finally neared the outskirts of Denver.

After the sun went down. The whippoorwills began their songs.

1. Prairie dogs greet each other in a strange way. By kissing.

2. Knights wore capes over their armor. Because their crests indicated that they would be valuable as hostages held for ransom.

3. The bottom of the ocean may be a dangerous place to dump nuclear waste. For scientists have detected the existence of violent storms on the ocean floor.

4. Mt. Vesuvius erupted on August 24, A.D. 79. Covering Pompeii, Herculaneum, and Stabiae with more than sixty feet of mud and ash.

5. The United States lost the America's Cup in 1983. Having successfully defended it since 1851.

6. Stretching the entire length of the continent. The Andes Mountains dominate the geography of western South America.

7. Once limited to the Western states. Rodeos now enjoy national popularity.

8. The word *Mississippi* probably comes from the Chippewa term *Mici zibi*. Which means "great river."

9. Although the *Star Wars* films have been immensely popular. They

have yet to attract the number of fans that still enjoy the *Star Trek* television series.

10. Country-western music is now more popular than any other musical style. Even more popular than the rock music that began in the 1950s.

4.3 Comma Splices; Fused Sentences

Comma splices and fused sentences can be corrected in four principal ways:

1. Use a period and write two separate sentences.
2. Use a semicolon between two independent clauses.
3. Use a comma and a coordinating conjunction between two independent clauses.
4. Make one of the clauses dependent.

■ *Indicate first whether each of the following is a comma splice or a fused sentence. Then, in correcting the sentence, indicate the method you used by writing one of the four above numbers in the blank.*

EXAMPLES

Kansas City calls itself the City of Fountains, its goal is to build a new public fountain every year. *;but* *Comma splice/2*

Death Valley, California, is now a desert it once was a large lake. *fused sentence/3*

1. Many think popcorn is a typical American food, actually it was popular in ancient times. _____

2. Ingmar Bergman directed *The Seventh Seal* in 1956, the next year he directed *Wild Strawberries*. _____

3. The surgeon made his morning rounds then he drove to his office. _____

4. Constant reading will improve your vocabulary it will also improve your writing. _____

5. Palindromes are groups of words that read the same forward or backward, they are difficult to compose. _____

6. Rome destroyed Carthage in 146 B.C. it occupied Egypt in A.D. 30. _____

7. Getting the right to vote is one thing, using it is another. _____

8. Many old cars use premium gasoline, which is

now difficult to find they can be tuned to use
regular or lower octane unleaded gasoline. _____

9. Scientists disagree on the source of intelligence,
   some say heredity is the main source, but others
   believe that the environment is more influential. _____

10. Norfolk, Phoenix, Philadelphia, Urbana, and
    Jacksonville are names of cities in five different
    states you can find towns bearing these names in
    New York State. _____

4.4 Comma Splices; Fused Sentences

■ *In the blanks to the right, indicate whether each of the following is a comma splice or a fused sentence. In correcting the sentence, indicate the method you used by writing one of these four numbers in the blank: (1) corrected with a period (two sentences); (2) corrected with a semicolon; (3) corrected with a comma and a coordinating conjunction; (4) corrected by making one of the clauses dependent.*

EXAMPLE

The huge jet left the airport at 11:00 P.M. it reached its destination at 6:00 P.M.   *fused sentence/2*

1. Mosquitoes are found in various climates they thrive in Alaska as well as in the tropics.   _____

2. Coast Guard cadets continue to train on sailing ships, thus they gain firsthand knowledge of traditional nautical lore.   _____

3. A New York law at the turn of the century regulated automobiles under an ordinance applied to cattle it required a person to walk in front of the automobile carrying a red flag or lantern.   _____

4. The Federal Reserve System controls the money supply for the entire United States local banks often borrow money from regional Reserve banks to ensure economic stability.   _____

5. In 1933, eighty million movie tickets were sold in America, in 1978, fewer than ten million were sold.   _____

6. One of the first commemorative stamps of 1981 honored Whitney Moore Young he founded the National Urban League.   _____

7. In 1983, the U.S. Commerce Department reported that the average salary in Alaska was $28,720 a year, this was over $15,000 more than the average salary in South Dakota that year.   _____

8. Dreams disturb our sleep often we wake in the middle of the night.   _____

9. The flash bulbs momentarily blinded the celebrity, he continued to smile and wave. _____

10. Heavy rains have slowed construction on the new high-rise, however, the project remains ahead of schedule. _____

NAME _____

DATE _____ SCORE _____

4.5 Sentence Fragments, Comma Splices, and Fused Sentences

■ *Revise the following paragraph to eliminate sentence fragments, comma splices, and fused sentences.*

For years, atmospheric scientists have studied the ozone layer over Antarctica. Hoping to discover why large holes in it appear every spring. They now believe they have the answer manmade chemicals seem to be the culprits. Perhaps even more troubling are the findings of a very recent study, it reveals that a hole in the ozone layer above the Arctic appears to be forming. Such studies begging for further research.

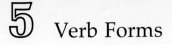

5   Verb Forms

VERBS

All verbs have three principal parts:

> the **infinitive** (*to concern*)
> the **past tense** (*concerned*)
> the **past participle** (*concerned*)

These principal parts are listed in the dictionary entry of each irregular verb.

Regular, Irregular Verbs

Verbs can be regular or irregular in form. **Regular verbs** (*add, help*) form the past tense and the past participle by adding *-d*, *-ed*, or sometimes *-t* (*kept, dreamt*). The principal parts of *add* and *help* are *add, added, added; help, helped, helped*.

Irregular verbs change form in the past tense and the past participle. Some irregular verbs (*begin, sing*) form the past tense and the past participle by changing a single vowel (*sing, sang, sung*). Other irregular verbs change more than one letter (*drive, drove, driven*).

Transitive, Intransitive Verbs

Verbs also can be **transitive** (take an object) or **intransitive** (do not take an object).

TRANSITIVE VERB
> The cook *tasted* the special *sauce*. (*Sauce* is the direct object.)

INTRANSITIVE VERB
> The rain *fell* on the roof. (*Fell* does not take an object.)

Especially troublesome are the irregular verbs *lie, lay; sit, set; rise, raise*. The verbs *lay, set*, and *raise* are transitive and take an object. The verbs *lie, sit*, and *rise* are intransitive and do not take an object.

Each of these verbs has a specific meaning. *Lie* means to recline or to be situated; *lay*, to place. *Sit* means to be seated; *set*, to place or arrange. *Rise* means to get up; *raise* means to lift. When trying to decide on the correct form of the verb, think of the meaning you want, whether the verb takes an object or not, the tense you need, and the correct principal part. (See also pp. 78–79.)

She *lays* the book on the table. (present tense of *lay*)

She *laid* the book on the table and left. (past tense of *lay*)

The boat *lies* in the harbor. (present tense of *lie*)

The boat *lay* in the harbor most of last week. (past tense of *lie*)

The waiter *set* the plate on the table. (*Plate* is the direct object.)

The archeologist *laid* the relics taken from the temple on the examining table. (*Relics* is the direct object.)

The honor guard will *raise* the flag. (*Flag* is the direct object.)

Some of the swimmers were *lying* on the beach. (*Lying* is intransitive and takes no object.)

The sewing basket was *sitting* in the corner. (*Sitting* is intransitive and takes no object.)

The speaker *rises* to address the meeting. (*Rises* is intransitive and takes no object.)

The principal parts of these verbs are included in the following list of difficult verbs.

Principal Parts of Some Troublesome Verbs

INFINTIVE	PAST TENSE	PAST PARTICIPLE
arise	arose	arisen
awake	awoke, awaked	awoke, awaked
be	was	been
bear (to carry)	bore	borne
bear (to give birth)	bore	born, borne
begin	began	begun
bid (offer)	bid	bid
bid (order or say)	bade	bidden
bite	bit	bitten, bit
blow	blew	blown
break	broke	broken
bring	brought	brought
burst	burst	burst
catch	caught	caught
choose	chose	chosen
come	came	come
deal	dealt	dealt
dig	dug	dug
dive	dived, dove	dived
do	did	done
drag	dragged	dragged
draw	drew	drawn
dream	dreamed, dreamt	dreamed, dreamt
drink	drank	drunk
drive	drove	driven
drown	drowned	drowned
eat	ate	eaten
fall	fell	fallen

INFINITIVE	PAST TENSE	PAST PARTICIPLE
find	found	found
flee	fled	fled
fly	flew	flown
forget	forgot	forgotten, forgot
freeze	froze	frozen
get	got	got, gotten
give	gave	given
go	went	gone
grow	grew	grown
hang (to execute)	hanged	hanged
hang (to suspend)	hung	hung
have	had	had
hear	heard	heard
know	knew	known
lay	laid	laid
lead	led	led
lend	lent	lent
let	let	let
lie	lay	lain
light	lighted, lit	lighted, lit
lose	lost	lost
pay	paid	paid
pay (rope)	payed	payed
plead	pleaded, pled	pleaded, pled
prove	proved	proven, proved
raise	raised	raised
ride	rode	ridden
ring	rang, rung	rung
rise	rose	risen
run	ran	run
say	said	said
see	saw	seen
set	set	set
shine (to give light)	shone	shone
shine (to polish)	shined	shined
show	showed	shown, showed
shrink	shrank, shrunk	shrunk
sing	sang, sung	sung
sink	sank, sunk	sunk
sit	sat	sat
slide	slid	slid
sow	sowed	sown, sowed
speak	spoke	spoken
spit	spit, spat	spit, spat
spring	sprang, sprung	sprung
stand	stood	stood
steal	stole	stolen
stink	stank, stunk	stunk
swim	swam, swum	swum
swing	swung	swung
take	took	taken
tear	tore	torn

5.1 Verb Forms

■ *Circle the correct verb form. Remember that intransitive verbs do not take direct objects. Remember that transitive verbs do take direct objects. Look for both the meaning and the tense of the verb.*

EXAMPLES

I cannot remember where I (lay, (laid)) my grocery list. (The verb *laid*, the past tense of *lay*, is transitive and takes the direct object *list*.)

The wind has (rose, (risen)) and the leaves have (flew, (flown)) everywhere. (*Risen* and *flown* are intransitive; they have no direct objects.)

How many pancakes have you (ate, (eaten))?

1. The lazy dog (lay, laid) on the sun-dappled porch for hours.

2. The shipwrecked sailors had not (ate, eaten) for days when their rescuers finally arrived.

3. Many are (took, taken) aback by his brashness.

4. Historians continue to write about the suffering that was (born, borne) by pioneers who were part of the settling of the West.

5. The glass collection was (shown, showed) at the museum.

6. Bobcats often (sit, set) in high places to observe their territories in safety.

7. Until the storm subsided and the sea became calm, all passengers had (laid, lain) in their berths.

8. The hitter chose to (lay, lie) the bat on his shoulder and hope for a walk.

9. Animals often (sit, set) in mud to cool their dry skin and to protect themselves from insects.

10. Hungry and exhausted, the fortress's weary defenders (rose, raised) the white flag of surrender.

5.2 Verb Forms

■ *Circle the correct verb form.*

EXAMPLE

It (taken, (took)) her several years to achieve her career goal.

1. Catching the terrified faces of each figure, Goya (froze, frozed) a brutal moment in his country's history in a memorable painting.

2. The new deodorant was (chose, chosen) by 30 percent of the people sampled.

3. During the presidential election campaign of 1952, several dissenting groups (breaked, broke) from the Democratic party.

4. A combination of dry grass, strong winds, and electrical storms or human carelessness has caused brush fires that have (rage, raged) for weeks.

5. People who lack ambition often wake up one day and realize that they have (sleeped, slept) away the best parts of their lives.

6. The candidate (begun, began) the campaign for Congress with an old-fashioned fish fry.

7. The Christmas shopper had (gave, given) storefront solicitors her last bit of change before she arrived home.

8. The rock (slided, slid) down the mountain.

9. Michael (set, sat) the groceries on the kitchen counter before he answered the telephone.

10. To prevent pipes from (busting, bursting) on wintry nights, one should turn on outside spigots.

5.3 Verb Forms

■ *Circle the correct verb form.*

EXAMPLE
Most art students have (prepare, (prepared)) a portfolio by the time they graduate from college.

1. The harvest moon (shined, shone) brightly over the peaceful autumn landscape.

2. The diplomat's preliminary discussions (lay, laid) the foundations for future talks.

3. Complaints about the unhealthy working conditions in the plant were (writed, written) down by the employees and submitted to the section manager.

4. When we tried out the appliance that we ordered through a television commercial, nothing (seem, seemed) to work right.

5. The cowboys on the cattle drive had (rode, ridden) over four hundred miles.

6. Donkeys have been known to (bore, bear) twice their weight on their exceptionally strong backs.

7. The school board (came, come) to no decision on the issue of attendance regulations.

8. A newly discovered Roman vessel (sanked, sank) off the coast of Sicily sometime during the third century B.C.

9. The first adhesive U.S. postage stamps were (issue, issued) on July 1, 1847.

10. In 1860, twenty thousand shoeworkers in New England (striked, struck), winning higher wages.

TENSE AND SEQUENCE OF TENSES

Use verbs carefully to express distinctions of time. Avoid needless shifts of tense.

Usually the **present tense** expresses present time.

> The architect *is designing* a new office complex.

It also may show repeated action.

> The architect *designs* office complexes.

The **past tense** shows past time.

> The architect *designed* a new office complex.
> I *lay* in the sun for an hour. (past tense of verb *lie*)

The **future tense** shows future time.

> I *shall go* home for lunch.

Perfect Tenses

The three perfect tenses are used in well-defined sequences. They indicate time or action completed before another time or action.

1. Use **present perfect** with present.

> I *have asked* her to help, and she *refuses*.

2. Use **past perfect** with past.

> He *had wanted* to diet, but he *could* not.

3. Use **future perfect** with future.

> He *will have finished* before we *will begin*.

Infinitive

An infinitive usually takes the present tense when it expresses action that occurs at the same time as that of the controlling verb.

> I *desired* to leave.

To *complete* the project, we *had* to work overtime yesterday.

Relationships between verbs should be logical and consistent.

NOT

I *walk* to the park and *had* lunch. (mixes present tense and past tense)

BUT

I *walked* to the park and *had* lunch. (past tense with past tense)

VOICE

When the subject acts, the verb is in the **active voice**. When the subject is acted upon, the verb is in the **passive voice**. Passive voice may lead to wordiness and can be confusing because it omits the doer of the action.

ACTIVE VOICE

We *will complete* the sales report by Wednesday. (*We* act.)

PASSIVE VOICE

The new sales report *will be completed* by Wednesday. (The *report* is acted upon.)

SUBJUNCTIVE MOOD

Use the **subjunctive mood** to show wishes, commands, or conditions contrary to fact.

I wish I *were* rich. (wish)

The rules require that we *be* silent. (command)

If I *were* vacationing this week, I would be a happy person. (condition contrary to fact)

5.4 Tense and Sequence of Tenses

■ *Correct the tense of the italicized verbs and verbals.*

EXAMPLES

plan

City planners consider an area's economic needs and ~~will plan~~ zoning laws.

went

We left the cabin and ~~go~~ for a walk.

1. When we went to the grocery store, we *pass* by our neighbor's office.

2. Good luck *came* when one least expects it.

3. Many people *had* asked an accountant for help with their income tax returns every year.

4. A press conference needs *to have been announced* as soon as the negotiations are completed.

5. The Connecticut River, the longest waterway in New England, *has drained* an area of 11,000 square miles as it flows from the Canadian border to Long Island Sound.

6. Most visitors to the National Museum of Art prefer *to have had* more time for their visit.

7. The *Constitution*, a forty-four-gun frigate of the U.S. Navy, had seen service in North Africa and in the War of 1812 before it *had been condemned* as unseaworthy in 1830.

8. Elephant herds haul away tons of silt from shallow water holes after their ritualistic herd baths; thus they *cleaned* the water and *created* water holes for other animals.

9. Fossil remains found in Antarctica *had linked* that continent with

South America and have provided further evidence that the two land masses were once connected.

10. The term "tailgate trombone" once referred to a New Orleans trombonist who *plays* while standing on the back of a horse-drawn parade cart.

5.5 Voice

■ *In the following sentences change the passive voice to active.*

EXAMPLES

Pride is instilled and friendships are promoted by voluntary neighborhood clean-up campaigns.

Voluntary neighborhood clean-up campaigns instill pride and promote friendship.

(*instilled* and *promoted* changed to action forms *instill* and *promote* with direct objects *pride* and *friendships*)

Parades are discouraged by the city council because many streets are under repair.

The city council discourages parades because many streets are under repair.

(*discouraged* changed to action form *discourages* with a direct object *parades*)

1. The first telephone conversation was held between Alexander Graham Bell and Thomas A. Watson on March 10, 1876.

_____

_____

2. Over one thousand people lost their lives when the *Lusitania*, a British steamer, was torpedoed by a German submarine on May 7, 1915.

_____

_____

3. A French army under Philip VI was defeated by English archers at the Battle of Crécy, the first important battle of the Hundred Years' War.

_____

_____

4. The aging actor was greeted by a few fans who still remembered him.

_____

_____

5. Last-minute changes were made on the movie set by the directors.

_____

_____

6. Both hoecake and hardtack were invented by chuck-wagon cooks on cattle drives, who rarely had time to construct ovens.

_____

_____

7. Flying squirrels are sighted commonly by visitors in the vast interior of the famous Okefenokee Swamp.

_____

_____

8. Flight 481 was cleared for take-off by the air traffic controller despite the heavy fog.

_____

_____

9. The roots of some American music have been traced by musicologists back to British, Scottish, Welsh, and Irish folk songs.

_____

_____

10. Fashions created by American designers are now bought by thousands of Europeans.

_____

_____

5.6 Verb Forms

■ *Rewrite the following paragraph, correcting all errors in verb tense and verb form.*

Ancient Greece produce many great political leaders, historians, philosophers, and scientists. Alexander the Great had spread Greek culture all the way to India. Herodotus writes the first historical work of Western civilization. Socrates, who never actually has written anything, nevertheless had a profound influence on future philosophers. Aristotle has given to the modern world biological classifications and a scientific approach that is requiring all theory to be base on observed facts. These great men not only shape our past; they will have continued to influenced our future.

Subject and Verb: Agreement

Use singular verbs with singular subjects, and use plural verbs with plural subjects. The *-s* or *-es* ending of the present tense of a verb in the third person (*he hopes, she stops*) indicates the singular. For most nouns, however, these same endings indicate the plural.

After Compound Subject

A compound subject with *and* usually takes a plural verb.

> Quiltwork *and* other traditional handicrafts *are* now considered folk art.

When compound subjects are joined by *or, either . . . or*, or *neither . . . nor*, the verb should agree with the subject closest to it.

> Neither the diagram nor the directions are easy to read.
> Neither the directions nor the diagram is easy to read.

Collective Nouns

Collective nouns (words like *family, flock, jury*) take a singular verb when referring to a group as a unit; they take a plural verb when the members of a group are treated individually.

> My *family is* going on a trip this weekend.
> My *family are* going to Hawaii, New Jersey, and Ohio on Labor Day.

After Relative Pronoun

After a relative pronoun (such as *who, which,* and *that*), the verb in the relative clause has the same person and number as the *antecedent* of the pronoun.

> Over half of the people who *work* in retail sales are women.

After Titles

A title of a book or film is singular and requires a singular verb, even if it contains plural words and ideas.

> *Elements of Films* is a useful book.

After *There, Here*

In sentences that begin with *there* and *here*, the verb agrees with the subject of the sentence.

> There *is* an old *mill* on this road. (*Mill* is the subject.)
>
> There *are* many *challenges* in this project. (*Challenges* is the subject.)

Word Groups

Word groups, such as *in addition to* and *as well as*, do not change the number of the subject when they separate the subject and the verb.

> State *officials as well as* our mayor *are examining* the problem.

The Subject

The subject of the sentence, not the predicate noun, determines the number of the verb.

> Her main *strength is* her ability to listen and to follow instructions.

When the subject in a sentence is *inverted*, the verb should agree with the *subject* of the sentence, not with the word that comes directly before the verb.

> At the party *were Beatrice* and her *sister*. (Plural verb agrees with compound subject.)

6.1 Subject and Verb Agreement

■ *Underline each subject once; then write the correct verb in the blank at the right.*

EXAMPLES

<u>Local banks</u> and <u>chambers of commerce</u> usually (provide, provides) useful information to new residents.

provide

Neither <u>the team members</u> nor <u>their coach</u> (expect, expects) a victory.

expects

1. Auto manufacturers recall thousands of cars each year because they discover that there (are, is) a major defect that could cause an accident. _____

2. There are more than 250 tributaries that (empties, empty) into the Mississippi River. _____

3. Visiting national parks and driving through small towns that are off main highways (is, are) favorite types of vacations for many people. _____

4. Neither Montezuma II nor his Aztec subjects (was, were) able to prevent Cortés's sacking of Tenochtitlán. _____

5. There (come, comes) a time when everyone must think about retirement. _____

6. A large crowd of people (was, were) at the sports arena. _____

7. We like everyone who (live, lives) in our neighborhood. _____

8. The convocation speaker as well as his wife and children (was, were) welcomed heartily by the audience. _____

9. Copper is one of the few metals that (appears, appear) in a pure form in nature. _____

10. There (is, are) many Americans who never bother to vote. _____

6.2 Subject and Verb Agreement

■ *Underline each subject once; then write the correct verb in the blank at the right.*

EXAMPLES

All <u>members</u> of the council (is, are) present.   *are*

<u>Everyone</u> (is, are) here for the presentation of the awards.   *is*

1. Only about forty of the two hundred different kinds of anapheles mosquitoes (carry, carries) malaria.   _____

2. Indiana as well as Wisconsin, Illinois, and Michigan (touches, touch) Lake Michigan.   _____

3. The majority of public officials (is, are) dedicated to their work.   _____

4. Not only gold but also silver, lead, copper, manganese, and arsenic (is, are) found in the mountains of Montana.   _____

5. Whoever (say, says) the new statue in the park is ugly is making an understatement.   _____

6. The Science Club, which is sponsored by the Physics Department, (participate, participates) in the state science fair this weekend.   _____

7. On the list of bowlers in the tournament (was, were) Mary Ashley, Sonja Taylor, and Ruthie Johns, clearly the best in the region.   _____

8. The mural, viewed at the shopping center by the opening-day crowd, (was, were) shocking to many.   _____

9. The desire to economize and help solve the energy shortage (sell, sells) many subcompact automobiles.   _____

10. Students' lack of desire to learn (cause, causes) teachers many heartaches.   _____

7 Pronouns: Agreement, Reference, and Usage

ANTECEDENTS

Use singular pronouns to refer to singular antecedents, and use plural pronouns to refer to plural antecedents. Use a plural pronoun to refer to compound antecedents, except in those cases where the antecedents refer to the same person.

> *Phyllis* asked the waiter to bring *her* check.
>
> *We* asked the waiter to bring *our* checks.

Which and *that* refer to animals and things. *Who* refers to people and rarely to animals and things called by name. *That* refers to animals and things but only occasionally to people.

> The refrigerator *that* (*which*) I bought never needs defrosting.
>
> The representative *who* sold it to me guaranteed the unit for ten years.

Pronouns should not refer vaguely to an entire sentence or to unidentified people. Do not make vague references using the pronouns *they, them, it, you, this,* or *which*.

> I have trouble taking standardized tests. *This* is my problem. (*This* is too vague.)
>
> *You* know that *they* will do *it* every time. (*You, they,* and *it* are vague references.)

Make a pronoun refer clearly to one antecedent only.

UNCERTAIN
> The man went to the doctor after *he* finished work. (Does *he* refer to *doctor* or *man?*)

CLEAR
> After *he* finished work, the man went to the doctor. (*He* now clearly refers to *man*.)

7.1 Pronouns: Agreement and Reference

■ *In the following sentences choose the correct pronouns and write them in the blanks at the right.*

EXAMPLES

The band dedicated the song to all (its, their) fans.

its

County maps are useful for census-takers as (they, he or she) attempt to reach all households.

they

1. Although the immediate causes of many severe allergic reactions is unknown, (it, they) can be determined later by tests.   _____

2. Freight trains were called *rattlers* in the 1840s because (it, they) made so much noise.   _____

3. In 1917, the French executed Dutch dancer Gertrud Margarete Zelle, (who, which) was better known as Mata Hari, because they were convinced she was spying for the Germans.   _____

4. The multinational corporation retained many lawyers to handle (their, its) legal affairs.   _____

5. People often accidentally find (themself, themselves) on a street that is dark and foreboding.   _____

6. Keeping (its, their) budget under control, the company was able to save several thousand dollars.   _____

7. Dana Morey and her assistants are turning (her, their) attention to more radical architectural designs.   _____

8. People who swim without supervision endanger (one's life; their lives).   _____

9. Large corporations in the United States (who, that) do international business hire college graduates with a knowledge of foreign languages.   _____

10. Many researchers are now studying the causes of heart failure to find ways to prevent (it, them).   _____

7.2 Pronouns: Agreement and Reference

■ *In the following sentences choose the correct pronouns and write them in the blanks at the right.*

EXAMPLE

All of the law students submitted (his, their, one's) reports today. *their*

1. The researchers working on sleep deprivation reported that (his or her, their) subjects became paranoid after several days without sleep. _____

2. Laying bricks takes patience and skill; (it requires, they require) a long apprenticeship. _____

3. Mahjongg, an ancient Chinese game played with 144 pieces, is so complicated that (its, their) players must often consult their rule books. _____

4. The well drillers finally found water at seven hundred feet, the greatest depth (it, they) had ever had to drill. _____

5. The committee submitted (its, their) revised budget. _____

6. The foremen discussed the new labor contract with (his, their) union members. _____

7. The lights went out in (their, they're) apartment. _____

8. Children often have imaginary friends to whom (they are, he is) especially attached. _____

9. Bloodhounds pick up the scent of lost people and follow (him, it). _____

10. In 1833, the population of Chicago, Illinois, was only 350, but within a century (it, they) numbered over three million. _____

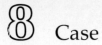 Case

Pronouns have three cases: subjective, possessive, and objective. Personal pronouns and the relative pronoun *who* are inflected for these cases.

Subjective (acting)—I, he, she, we, they, who, you, it

Possessive (possessing)—my (mine), your (yours), his, her (hers), its, our (ours), their (theirs), whose

Objective (acted upon)—me, him, her, us, them, one, whom, you, it

To determine case, find out how a word is used in its own clause—for example, whether it is a subject, a subjective complement, a possessive, or an object.

Use the **subjective case** for subjects and subjective complements.

SUBJECT
The contractor and *I* are about to reach an agreement. (Use *I*, not *me*, for the subject.)

SUBJECTIVE COMPLEMENT (OR PREDICATE NOMINATIVE)
The winner was *I*. (Use *I*, not *me*, afer a linking verb.)

Use the **possessive case** to show ownership and with gerunds.

Their work was complete. (ownership)

His constant *whistling* annoys his co-workers. (gerund)

The possessive forms of personal pronouns do *not* have apostrophes.

His is the best solution.

The possessive forms of indefinite pronouns (*everybody's, one's, anyone's*) do have apostrophes. Contractions such as *it's* (for *it is*) and *she's* (for *she is*) do have apostrophes.

Also use the **objective case** for the object of a preposition and for the subject of an infinitive.

Who among *us* will volunteer? (*Us* is the object of *among*.)

The college selected *her* to be the coach. (*Her* is the subject of the infinitive *to be*.)

For Interrogative Pronouns

The case of interrogatives (*who, whose, whom, what, which* used in questions) depends on their use in a specific clause.

Whom did you call about our new book orders? (Use *whom*, not *who*, because the interrogative pronoun is a direct object of *call*.)

For Appositives

For pronouns used as **appositives** (words that rename nouns or pronouns) use the same case as the noun or pronoun renamed.

SUBJECTIVE

> Only we—Sharon and I—were excused. (*Sharon* and *I* rename the subject *we*; hence, use *I*, not *me*.)

OBJECTIVE

> The instructor excused two of us—Sharon and *me*. (*Sharon* and *me* rename the object of the preposition *of*; hence, use the objective case.)

After *Than, As*

The correct case of a pronoun used after *than* or *as* is determined by completing the missing verb of the clause:

> Margaret is taller than I. (*Than I am* is the complete clause; *I* is the subject of the clause.)
>
> She worked harder than you or I. (*than you or I worked*)
>
> This crisis hurt him more than her. (*more than it hurt her; her* is the object)

8.1 Case

■ *Write the correct case form in the following sentences in the blanks at the right.*

EXAMPLES

(Whoever, Whomever) invented the wheel deserves the gratitude of everyone.

Whoever

(subject of verb *invented*)

About (whom, who) are you speaking?

whom

(object of preposition *about*)

1. Joseph Haydn was an Austrian composer (who, whom) developed the sonata form. _____

2. Richard, Doris, and (her, she) are planning to major in marine biology. _____

3. It was a pleasure to see (they, them) working hard for a change. _____

4. Herbert Hoover's mother, a traveling Quaker preacher, died when he was eight, leaving (he, him) and his brother as orphans. _____

5. The race was nearly a tie, and (who, whom) won it was difficult to determine. _____

6. The president gave (us, we) three special awards at the annual sales meeting. _____

7. No other typist in the class can type as rapidly as (he, him). _____

8. The band members asked (themselves, theirselves) what had gone wrong during the rehearsal. _____

9. We knew (her, she) to be loyal to her principles. _____

10. He dedicated his book to (whoever, whomever) cherished liberty. _____

8.2 Case

■ *Write the correct case form in the following sentences in the blanks at the right.*

EXAMPLE

(Their, Them) singing is delightful.   *Their*

(possessive case with gerund)

1. "We were delighted to hear about (you, your) winning the lottery," began the letter from the collection agency. _____

2. It was (he, him) who first proposed a change in office procedures. _____

3. Neither we nor (they, them) could recall the third labor of Hercules. _____

4. Our teacher thought that Ann and (I, me) were always in trouble. _____

5. Several tendons in (my, mine) leg were injured in the fall. _____

6. (Who, Whom) did the publisher decide to choose as the new editor? _____

7. Many Americans complain that (we, us) taxpayers must pay too much money to the government. _____

8. We helped more than (they, them), but they received more credit. _____

9. The governor traveled to France with my wife and (I, me) to celebrate Bastille Day. _____

10. (Whoever, Whomever) owns the disputed land near the present borders of Wyoming and Colorado may be wealthy someday. _____

NAME _____

DATE _____ SCORE _____

8.3 Pronoun Case and Pronoun Agreement

■ *Revise the following paragraph, correcting all errors in pronoun case and agreement.*

The Indians of Peru grow over four hundred varieties of potatoes. These Indians, most of who live in mountainous regions, prefer small varieties. It is easier and quicker to cook. Occasionally, some of they produce modern, larger varieties, but them are only for sale in urban markets. Most find the taste of older, smaller varieties to be better because it has less water and more fiber. Some agricultural consultants whom have worked in Peru recently admit that many older varieties are also more resistant to certain diseases.

⑨ Adjectives and Adverbs

ADJECTIVES AND ADVERBS COMPARED

Adjectives modify nouns and pronouns. **Adverbs** modify verbs, adjectives, and other adverbs.

> *The bright* light hurt *our* eyes. (*The* and *bright* are adjectives modifying *light,* and *our* is a possessive adjective modifying *eyes.*)
>
> The news spread *quickly.* (*Quickly* is an adverb modifying *spread.*)

Most adverbs end in *-ly.* Only a few adjectives (*Lovely, friendly,* for example) have this ending. Some adverbs have two forms, one with *-ly* and one without (*closely, close* and *quickly, quick*). Most adverbs are formed by adding *-ly* to adjectives (*sudden, suddenly* and *hasty, hastily.*)

> We had an *easy* choice to make. (*Easy* is an adjective.)
>
> We made the choice *easily.* (*Easily* is an adverb.)

Use a predicate adjective, not an adverb, after a linking verb, such as *be, become, seem, look, appear, feel, sound, smell, taste.*

> The *laundry* is *dry.* (*Dry* describes the *laundry.*)
>
> The *tire* looked *flat.* (*Flat* describes the *tire.*)
>
> The *pie* smells *delicious.* (*Delicious* describes how the *pie* smells.)
>
> The gymnast performed *well.* (The adverb *well* modifies the verb *performed.*)

FORMS OF THE COMPARATIVE AND SUPERLATIVE

Use the **comparative form** of the adjective to refer to two things; use the **superlative form** to refer to more than two. Add *-er* or *-est* to form the comparative and the superlative of most short modifiers.

> The new air terminal is much *larger* than the old one.
>
> Of the five hotels in our city, the *newest* one is the *largest.*

Use *more* or *most* (or *less* or *least*) rather than *-er* and *-est* before long modifiers, that is, modifiers of several syllables.

> She is *more capable* than her sister (not *capabler*)
>
> She is the *most capable* person I know. (not *capablest*)
>
> He is very *fast.* (predicate adjective)
>
> He is *faster* than his brother. (comparative form)
>
> He is the *fastest* runner in our class. (superlative form)

Some adjectives and adverbs have irregular comparative and superlative forms:

good, better, best; bad, worse, worst

NOTE: Some adjectives imply an absolute state and cannot be intensified.

NOT

Her ideas are very unique.

BUT

Her ideas are unique.

9.1 Adjective or Adverb?

■ *Write the correct form of the adjective or adverb in the blank at the right.*

EXAMPLES

The angry customer spoke (rapid, rapidly).   *rapidly*

(adverb *rapidly* modifies verb *spoke*)

(Slight, Slightly) sunlight is enough for this fern.   *Slight*

(adjective *slight* modifies noun *sunlight*)

1. The work went (well, good) after the construction crew was enlarged.   _____

2. The nations of the British Commonwealth are not always tied (close, closely) to the British crown.   _____

3. Most wild animals fight (vicious, viciously) when they are cornered.   _____

4. A Statue of Vulcan stands (high, highly) over Birmingham, Alabama, as a symbol of that city's large steel industry.   _____

5. Before the meetings began, the members of the trade commission from England were greeted very (warm, warmly).   _____

6. After deciding which college to attend, she felt (good, well) about her decision.   _____

7. Every applicant performed (good, well) on the tests.   _____

8. The region of Brittany is (considerable, considerably) different from the rest of France.   _____

9. The plain before the pioneers was (vast, vastly) and covered with wildflowers.   _____

10. (Really, Real) good ice cream is now available in over fifty flavors and at a reasonable cost.   _____

11. Teams that remain (close, closely) are usually very successful.   _____

12. The defense attorney argued his client's case (energetic, energetically) before the jury. _____

13. The newscaster told the anxious audience that the rescue was going as (good, well) as could be expected. _____

14. The Western Hemisphere has two of the world's (larger, largest) rivers, the Amazon and the Mississippi; of the two, the Amazon is the (larger, largest), but the Mississippi is the (most, more) important economically. _____

15. Once on the endangered species list, the American alligator is now (abundant, abundantly) because of (more strict, stricter) law enforcement and better game management. _____

16. The aging actress appeared quite (youthful, youthfully) in her latest film. _____

17. Of all the space walks, Armstrong's was the (better, best). _____

18. The stock cars passed the stands so (rapidly, rapid) that it was impossible to tell (accurate, accurately) who was ahead. _____

19. Being (solid, solidly) behind the new housing program, the young politicians had to fight opponents who were (strong, strongly) opposed to them. _____

20. Most conductors are (usual, usually) pleased with requests for encores. _____

9.2 Adjective or Adverb?

■ *Write the correct form of the adjective or adverb in the blank at the right.*

EXAMPLES

The soprano sings very (good, well).   _*well*_

(adverb *well* modifies *sings*)

The clarinet solo sounded especially (well, good).   _*good*_

(adjective *good* after linking verb)

1. Spelunkers must crawl (cautious, cautiously) through caves.   _____

2. The spectators cheered (loud, loudly) when the basketball player shot the ball from half court.   _____

3. (Normal, Normally) many employees expect to leave early on Friday.   _____

4. Alfred Hitchcock's *Psycho* is (some, somewhat) more highly acclaimed than *Rear Window*, a movie he produced many years before.   _____

5. The extra work caused by the reduction in the department's staff fell (heavy, heavily) on the shoulders of four employees.   _____

6. Trent tried to complete his homework as (quick, quickly) as possible.   _____

7. "If you want a (real, really) effective stereo that plays music (clear, clearly)," the clerk advised, "buy a graphic equalizer."   _____

8. After the relay race, the losing team looked (glum, glumly) and said that they felt (worse, worst, worser, badder) than they looked.   _____

9. As the cowboy (careful, carefully) put his cup of very thick coffee down, he remarked to the waitress, "One thing about your coffee: it sure packs a wallop."   _____

10. On Halloween, most children are (real, really) afraid to enter cemeteries or abandoned houses. _____

9.3 Comparative and Superlative

■ *Write the correct form of the comparative or superlative in the blanks.*

EXAMPLES

controversial Boxing is probably the *most controversial* of all major sports.

funny The comedian's latest routine is *funnier* than his last one.

1. original This is the _____ marketing concept that this department has ever considered.

2. populous Belize is _____ than any other Central American nation.

3. serious Reckless driving is a _____ traffic offense than is speeding.

4. visible The northern lights are _____ in Alaska than in the forty-eight contiguous states.

5. tall The _____ mountain peaks in the Western Hemisphere are in the Andes.

6. great The Klondike region of the Yukon was the site of the _____ gold rush the world has ever known.

7. easy It is _____ to grow blueberries in acidic, damp, but well-drained soils than in dry, alkaline soils.

8. little Jean Lafitte's role in the defense of New Orleans during the War of 1812 is _____ understood than Andrew Jackson's.

9. large Norway is _____ than the state of Utah.

10. long If Norway's coastline were straight, it would stretch 12,500 miles, _____ than that of any other Scandinavian country.

9.4 Adjectives and Adverbs: Review

■ *Write a paragraph on a topic of your choice. Include at least five adjectives and five adverbs. Underline the adjectives once, the adverbs twice.*

_____

_____

_____

_____

_____

_____

_____

_____

_____

_____

_____

SENTENCE STRUCTURE

10 Coordination, Subordination, Completeness, Comparisons, and Consistency

Linking a number of short independent clauses and sentences produces wordiness and monotony and fails to show precise relationships between thoughts.

EXAMPLE

The United States has changed significantly in the last fifty years, for the life expectancy of Americans has increased ten years for men and fifteen years for women, and the nation's work force has quadrupled.

IMPROVED

The United States has changed significantly in the last fifty years. The life expectancy of Americans has increased ten years for men and fifteen years for women. In addition, the nation's work force has quadrupled.

SUBORDINATION

Use subordinate clauses accurately and effectively to avoid excessive coordination and to achieve variety and proper emphasis. However, avoid excessive subordination, which results in long and monotonous sentences.

EXCESSIVE SUBORDINATION

My grandfather took great pleasure throughout his life in the craft of carving wooden figures, which he learned to do when he was young, which was a time when people did not have the great number of amusements that we have today.

BETTER

My grandfather, who lived in a time when people did not have the great number of amusements of today, learned when young to carve wooden figures. He took great pleasure in the craft throughout his life.

Express main ideas in independent clauses; express less important ideas in subordinate clauses.

IMPROPER SUBORDINATION

Few people know that he got his seed from mills that made apple cider, although Johnny Appleseed became famous for planting apple trees throughout the Ohio Valley.

BETTER

Although few people know that he got his seed from mills that made apple cider, Johnny Appleseed became famous for planting apple trees throughout the Ohio Valley.

118

Avoid excessive overlapping of subordinate clauses. A series of clauses in which each one depends on the previous one is confusing.

OVERLAPPING SUBORDINATION

> The United States Treasury Department, which is located in Washington, which is responsible for the printing and minting of currency, is also responsible for the protection of the President.

IMPROVED

> Located in Washington, the United States Treasury Department is responsible for the printing and minting of currency and for the protection of the President.

COMPLETENESS

After *So, Such, Too*

Make your sentences complete in structure and thought, especially sentences with *so, such,* and *too.*

NOT CLEAR

> The storm was so violent. (So violent that what happened?)

CLEAR

> The storm was so violent that we closed all the shutters.

NOT CLEAR

> The secretary was too busy. (Too busy to do what?)

CLEAR

> The secretary was too busy to answer the telephone.

Omission of Verbs and Prepositions

Do not omit a verb or a preposition that is necessary to the structure of the sentence.

NOT

> We were interested and then bored by the lecture.

BUT

> We were interested in and then bored by the lecture.

NOT

> The passengers were impatient and the plane late.

BUT

> The passengers were impatient, and the plane was late.

Omission of *That*

The omission of *that* is often confusing.

INCOMPLETE

> He was grieved she did not love him.

He was grieved that she did not love him.

COMPARISONS

Make comparisons clear and complete by comparing only similar terms, using the word *other* where necessary and avoiding awkward and incomplete comparisons.

INCORRECT

The bite of a person is often worse than a dog.

LOGICAL

The bite of a person is often worse than the bite of a dog.

INCORRECT

The Grand Canyon is larger than any canyon in the world.

LOGICAL

The Grand Canyon is larger than any other canyon in the world.

INCORRECT

Reading is one of the most pleasant if not the most pleasant pastime one can enjoy. (After *one of the most pleasant*, the plural, *pastimes*, is required.)

BETTER

Reading is one of the most pleasant pastimes one can enjoy, if not the most pleasant.

OR

Reading is one of the most pleasant pastimes.

Avoid ambiguous comparisons.

AMBIGUOUS

We enjoyed visiting the city more than our parents. (*More* than visiting parents, or *more* than the parents enjoyed the city?)

CLEAR

We enjoyed visiting the city more than our parents did.

CONSISTENCY

Avoid confusing shifts in grammatical forms.

Shifts in Tense

INCORRECT

The doctor was well trained, but his patients are dissatisfied.

CORRECT

The doctor is well trained, but his patients are dissatisfied.

120

Shifts in Person

INCORRECT

When we flew over St. Louis, you could see the Mississippi River.

CORRECT

When we flew over St. Louis, we could see the Mississippi River.

Shifts in Number

INCORRECT

A person may decide on their vocation late in life.

CORRECT

People may decide on their vocations late in life.

Shifts in Voice

INCORRECT

The assignment *is read* by the student, and then she *answers* the questions at the end of the chapter.

CORRECT

The student *reads* the assignment, and then she *answers* the questions at the end of the chapter. (Put both parts of the sentence in the active voice.)

10.1 Excessive Coordination

Sentences should be varied in length, structure, and emphasis. Coordination, subordination, parallelism, and word order should show relationships precisely and emphasize important elements of thought. Do not string together a number of short independent clauses; excessive coordination fails to show precise relationships between thoughts.

■ *Rewrite the following sentences to eliminate excessive coordination.*

EXAMPLE
The election results are close and both candidates declared victory, so the officials decided to recount the ballots.

Because the election results were close and both candidates declared victory, the officials decided to recount the ballots.

1. The campers located a good campsite, and they pitched their tents, and then they built a campfire.

_____

_____

_____

2. The portrait artist carefully mixed the pigments, and he prepared to finish painting the facial features, and his subject sat patiently.

_____

_____

_____

3. Our retirement check arrived today, and we deposited it, and we began our vacation.

_____

_____

_____

4. *The Jazz Singer* opened on October 5, 1927, it was the first sound film, and Al Jolson played the leading role.

_____

_____

_____

5. The water cascaded over the falls, and we watched the salmon leaping into the air, and we wondered what compelled them to such struggle.

_____

_____

_____

6. The old-fashioned fairy tales were frightening, and they were intended to be, and children heard them and were likely to stay on the path in the woods or near home, so the stories taught safety.

_____

_____

_____

7. The bazooka was an antitank weapon, and it was developed during World War II, but its name came from an odd musical instrument that was created by a popular comedian of the 1940s.

_____

_____

_____

8. Sunspots were discovered in the eighteenth century, and they have remained a mystery for two centuries, but now scientists are beginning to understand these solar phenomena.

_____

_____

_____

9. Some parents do not listen to their children, and they do not encourage them to talk; consequently, their children are not easily able to express their fears verbally, and they cannot talk about their hostilities.

_____

_____

_____

10. Lake Nicaragua was cut off from the Pacific Ocean by lava; it is ninety-six miles long and thirty-nine miles wide, and it is the only freshwater lake in the world to contain man-eating sharks.

_____

_____

_____

10.2 Subordination

■ *Indicate which sentence in each of the following pairs is preferable because the writer either uses proper subordination or eliminates excessive coordination.*

EXAMPLE

_a_   a. In the Southwest one can visit prehistoric cliff dwellings, which were built into canyon walls.

      b. In the Southwest one can visit, which were built into canyon walls, prehistoric cliff dwellings.

_____ 1. a. Although Admiral Nelson was severely wounded in the Battle of Trafalgar, he lived long enough to learn of the British victory.

        b. Admiral Nelson lived long enough to learn of the British victory, although he was severely wounded in the Battle of Trafalgar.

_____ 2. a. Thomas Nast was a famous political cartoonist, and he originated the Republican elephant and the Democratic donkey, and he is also credited with creating the modern depiction of Santa Claus.

        b. Thomas Nast, the famous political cartoonist who originated the Republican elephant and the Democratic donkey, is also credited with creating the modern depiction of Santa Claus.

_____ 3. a. Charlie had a small piece of cake after dinner although it was not on his diet.

        b. Although cake was not on his diet, Charlie had a small piece after dinner.

_____ 4. a. Winona traveled to Hawaii, when she stayed at a hotel near Diamond Head.

        b. Winona stayed at a hotel near Diamond Head when she traveled to Hawaii.

_____ 5. a. Entitled *Dafne*, the first opera, although it has been lost, was produced in 1597.

        b. Although the first opera, *Dafne*, has been lost, it was produced in 1597.

_____ 6. a. Apple pie has been more popular since the end of the eighteenth century, although pumpkin pie was served a century earlier.

b. Although pumpkin pie was served a century earlier, apple pie has been more popular since the end of the eighteenth century.

_____ 7. a. In 1803 Thomas Jefferson purchased the Louisiana Territory, which contained over fifty million acres of hardwood forest that has now been reduced to 3.5 million acres.

b. When Thomas Jefferson purchased the Louisiana Territory in 1803, it contained over fifty million acres of hardwood forest, which has now been reduced to 3.5 million acres.

_____ 8. a. The CDC is a federal agency, and it has the responsibility to diagnose and trace the sources of infectious diseases, and it is located in Atlanta, Georgia.

b. The CDC, which is a federal agency responsible for diagnosing and tracing the sources of infectious diseases, is located in Atlanta, Georgia.

_____ 9. a. The store manager had discussed several changes in company policy, and he asked for questions, and then he listened intently to what the employees said.

b. After the store manager had discussed several changes in company policy and asked for questions, he then listened intently to what the employees said.

_____ 10. a. The first American gold rush took place in Dahlonega, Georgia, in 1828, but there have been many gold rushes in the United States, and some have had greater historical impact.

b. Although there have been many gold rushes in the United States of greater historical impact, the first one took place in Dahlonega, Georgia, in 1828.

10.3 Subordination

■ *Revise the following sentences to achieve effective subordination.*

EXAMPLE

Mosquitoes can transmit diseases, and many communities spray to kill them.

Because mosquitoes can transmit diseases, many communities spray to kill them.

1. Many television stations in the United States are on the air twenty-four hours a day, but in many foreign countries the number of broadcasting hours is regulated carefully.

   _____

   _____

   _____

   _____

2. Microcomputers continue to grow in popularity, and many people attribute this popularity to their increasing capabilities.

   _____

   _____

   _____

   _____

3. The incidents of industrial theft are increasing, and many companies are installing elaborate security systems.

   _____

   _____

   _____

   _____

4. Radio was a popular form of entertainment in the 1930s and 1940s, and many people thought television would be useful only for educational and public-information programs.

_____

_____

_____

_____

5. Clare Boothe Luce was the first woman to represent the United States in a major diplomatic post, and she also served two terms in Congress.

_____

_____

_____

_____

6. Elaine was an industrious employee who was soon to be promoted to a position in management and who was studying accounting at a local college.

_____

_____

_____

_____

7. Many people did not understand the meaning of such terms as "head of household" and "parochial" on the 1970 census form, and so terms were made simpler on the 1980 census form.

_____

_____

_____

_____

8. Orson Welles is best known for his production of *Citizen Kane*, and he was twenty-six when he directed it.

_____

_____

_____

_____

9. Flamingos are large birds that wade in search of food and have red or pink plumage and have long legs, long necks, and a bill that turns downward at the tip.

_____

_____

_____

_____

10. A justice of the peace is a magistrate at the lowest level of a state's court system who performs marriages, who administers oaths, and who usually makes decisions about minor offenses that otherwise would crowd the dockets of higher courts.

_____

_____

_____

_____

10.4 Completeness and Comparisons

■ *Revise the following sentences to correct any errors in completeness and comparisons.*

EXAMPLES

The old warehouse is too small.

The old warehouse is too small to hold the inventory.

Rafting on the Colorado River is more exciting than any river in the United States.

Rafting is more exciting on the Colorado River than on any other river in the United States.

1. The advertisement claimed that the new detergent was twice as strong.

_____

_____

2. The climate in Arizona is better year-round.

_____

_____

3. The aircraft flying over the neighborhood have and continue to annoy residents.

_____

_____

_____

4. Joyce thinks her new pickup truck is better.

_____

_____

_____

5. Even casual viewers realize that Japanese kabuki theater is different.

_____

_____

_____

6. Forgetting a school assignment is worse than any mistake in school.

_____

_____

_____

7. The tenant in the apartment was both interested and suspicious of his neighbor.

_____

_____

_____

8. The new investigative reporter was as good if not better than some of the older reporters.

_____

_____

_____

9. The new play at our local theater is one of the most interesting if not the most interesting this season.

_____

_____

_____

10. My date liked me better than my friend Jane.

_____

_____

_____

10.5 Completeness and Comparisons

■ *Revise the following sentences to correct any errors in completeness and comparisons.*

EXAMPLE
No one works harder.

No one works harder than John.

1. In many cases laser surgery is more efficient.

   _____

   _____

   _____

2. The library staff worked harder this year.

   _____

   _____

   _____

3. Most people agree that Daylight Savings Time is better.

   _____

   _____

   _____

4. A completely rebuilt engine is usually just as dependable.

   _____

   _____

   _____

5. Most listeners recognize the tone of the alto saxophone more easily than the baritone saxophone.

   _____

6. The lawyer was both involved and concerned about the trial's outcome.

_____

_____

_____

7. For children, simple building blocks are as enjoyable if not more enjoyable than more expensive toys.

_____

_____

_____

8. Paraguay is twice as large but only slightly more populous than Uruguay.

_____

_____

_____

9. The clerk had never and never would be eligible for a long vacation because he took so many days off during the year.

_____

_____

_____

10. Sri Lanka, formerly Ceylon, has and continues to be the world's chief supplier of natural cinnamon.

_____

_____

_____

10.6 Consistency

■ *Revise the following sentences in order to make them structurally consistent. Avoid unnecessary shifts in tense, person, mood, or voice and shifts from one relative pronoun to another.*

EXAMPLES

Visibility was restricted to fifty feet when the airplane tries to take off.

Visibility was restricted to fifty feet when the airplane tried to take off.

(revised for consistency in tense)

When I traveled to the mountains of the Northwest, you can see great varieties of plant life.

When I traveled to the mountains of the Northwest, I saw great varieties of plant life.

(revised for consistency in person and tense)

1. I enjoy a cold glass of iced tea because one feels refreshed after you drink it.

_____

_____

2. When the fireworks display began, the onlookers could not hear yourself think.

_____

_____

3. We thought the light at the end of the tunnel is a sign of hope, but it was just a train coming in our direction.

_____

_____

_____

4. Dreams are not necessarily accidental, for they often were considered efforts of the subconscious to work out real problems.

_____

_____

5. Although the water table is higher this year than last, many lakes had still not regained their usual level.

_____

_____

6. The cheetah is very tired after chasing its quarry and usually rested for several minutes before it ate.

_____

_____

7. The woman discovered the real identity of her friend after she knows her for twenty years.

_____

_____

8. After we had been hiking for several days, we grow tired and stop to rest.

_____

_____

9. Before a person travels to the Rocky Mountains, they need to make sure their car's brakes are in sound condition.

_____

_____

10. The dam would have held huge amounts of water and will provide irrigation for the hundreds of farms in the nearby valley.

_____

_____

10.7 Sentence Structure: Review 1

■ *Revise the following paragraph, supplying any missing words and correcting all incomplete comparisons, shifts in person, mood, or tense, and excessive subordination.*

Whales, earth's largest living creatures, are of two types. Baleen whales, which eat tiny shrimp and other crustaceans and which include the relatively small California gray whale, which grows to be nearly forty-five feet long, as well as the blue whale, which grows to be over one hundred feet long, do not have teeth. You could find a variety of these whales in every ocean of the earth. The other great family of whales have teeth. Sperm whales, killer whales, narwhals, belugas, and porpoises belong to this group. Some of these species are endangered, and others not.

11 Position of Modifiers, Separation of Elements, Parallelism, and Sentence Variety

MODIFIERS

Attach modifiers to the correct word or element in the sentence to avoid confusion. Most adjectives precede the noun they modify. Adverbs may come before or follow the words they modify. Prepositional phrases usually follow the word they modify, as do adjective clauses. Adverbial phrases and clauses can be placed in various positions.

EXAMPLES

The new forms are finished. (adjective before the noun)

The auditions *soon* ended. (adverb before the verb)

The auditions ended *soon*. (adverb after the verb)

The officer *on the corner* hailed a motorist. (prepositional phrase modifying *officer*)

The lady came *to the door*. (prepositional phrase modifying *came*)

Sooner than we expected, the movie ended. (adverbial clause modifying *ended*)

The movie ended *sooner than we expected*. (adverbial clause modifying *ended*)

DANGLING MODIFIERS

Avoid dangling modifiers. A verbal phrase at the beginning of a sentence should logically modify the subject.

Dangling Participle

UNCLEAR

Seeing the whales surface nearby, my excitement grew.

CLEAR

Seeing the whales surface nearby, I became excited.

Dangling Gerund

UNCLEAR

After walking to the bus stop, my breath was short.

CLEAR

After walking to the bus stop, I was short of breath.

Dangling Infinitive

UNCLEAR

> To get an early start, *the alarm clock* was set for 6 A.M.

CLEAR

> To get an early start, *I set* the alarm clock for 6 A.M.

Dangling Prepositional Phrase

UNCLEAR

> While *in school*, my mother did her shopping.

CORRECT

> While *I was* in school, my mother did her shopping.

MISPLACED MODIFIERS, SQUINTING MODIFIERS

Almost any modifier that comes between an adjective clause and the word it modifies can cause confusion.

UNCLEAR

> Many people are questioned by grand juries *who may be innocent*.

CLEAR

> Many people *who may be innocent* are questioned by grand juries.

A modifier placed between two words so that it can modify either word is a **squinting modifier**.

UNCLEAR

> The chess master who was playing *calmly* won the first game.

CLEAR

> The chess master who was *calmly* playing won the first game.

SEPARATION OF ELEMENTS

Do not separate closely related elements, such as the subject and the verb, parts of a verb phrase, or a verb and an object.

AWKWARD

> The construction workers *had*, for a week, *expected* a new contract.

IMPROVED

> For a week, the construction workers *had expected* a new contract.

Avoid **split infinitives** (modifiers between *to* and the verb form).

NOT

> *to* actively *pursue*

BUT

> *to pursue* actively

142

PARALLELISM

Make constructions in a sentence parallel (balanced) by matching phrase with phrase, clause with clause, verb with verb, and so on.

FAULTY

The men argued *bitterly* and *were loud*.

IMPROVED

The men argued *bitterly* and *loudly*.

Repeat an article (*a, an,* or *the*), a preposition (*by, in, for,* and so on), or other words to preserve parallelism and clarity.

FAULTY

The aircraft was *in a storm* and *trouble*.

IMPROVED

The aircraft was *in a storm* and *in trouble*.

SENTENCE VARIETY

Vary sentences in structure and order. Use loose, periodic, balanced, and inverted sentence forms.

A **loose sentence** makes its main point at the beginning of the sentence and then adds qualifications or refinements.

We left early, missing the heavy traffic.

A **periodic sentence** saves the main point until the end of a sentence to create suspense or emphasis.

After a long afternoon visiting my aunt, I was exhausted.

A **balanced sentence** has parallel parts in terms of structure, length, and thoughts.

We must work so that we may live, not live so that we may work.

An **inverted sentence** reverses the usual subject-verb-object or subject-verb-complement order of declarative sentences.

Incalculable are the thoughts of infants.

11.1 Position of Modifiers

■ *Revise the following sentences to correct faulty modifiers.*

EXAMPLE

Some of the reporters were insistent who questioned the candidate.

Some of the reporters who questioned the candidate were insistent.

1. The harried commuters ran toward the buses with determined faces.

_____

_____

2. Many vacationers visit Glacier National Park to see its impressive mountain scenery each year.

_____

_____

3. The contract was signed today with the added clauses.

_____

_____

4. In 1819, the United States bought Florida wisely from Spain for five million dollars.

_____

_____

5. The community voted to turn a wooded area into a city park recently.

_____

_____

6. Suddenly reaching an arm through the bars of the cage, the man's pocket was torn by the monkey.

_____

_____

_____

7. The motorcyclist turned sharply right effortlessly missing the barrier on the race track.

_____

_____

_____

8. At the crossing the train passed by the auto pulling fifty boxcars and a caboose.

_____

_____

_____

9. Pedestrians stepped in the cement walking across the new sidewalk.

_____

_____

_____

10. The band marched down the street proudly showing off their new uniforms.

_____

_____

_____

11.2 Position of Modifiers

■ *Revise the following sentences to correct faulty modifiers.*

EXAMPLE

The air traffic controller who worked cautiously brought in Flight 89.

Working cautiously, the air traffic controller brought in Flight 89.

(corrected for a squinting modifier)

1. Peering deeply into the crystal ball, the skeptical man's future was predicted by the old gypsy woman.

_____

_____

_____

2. Before being tested, the engineer brought the experimental equipment to the laboratory.

_____

_____

_____

3. Racing across the field, I saw the left fielder make an astounding catch.

_____

_____

_____

4. People can hear Americans who speak Gullah, an English-African dialect, visiting the South Carolina and Georgia coasts.

_____

_____

_____

5. With two additional secretaries, the judge's crowded days were made easier.

_____

_____

_____

6. Receiving a substantial raise, the worker's house could be repaired.

_____

_____

_____

7. The secretary typed the letter using the office's newest electric typewriter.

_____

_____

_____

8. Performing aerobic exercises regularly contributes to good health.

_____

_____

_____

9. Television stations that run too many old movies frequently lose viewers.

_____

_____

_____

10. Many people prefer indirectly to make a point.

_____

_____

_____

11.3 Separation of Elements

■ *Do not separate closely related elements unnecessarily. Separation of parts of a verb phrase, a verb and its object, or a subject and its verb can be awkward or misleading. Revise the following sentences by correcting unnecessarily separated elements.*

EXAMPLE

Yellowstone Park, for many years, has been known as the site of Old Faithful.

For many years, Yellowstone Park has been known as the site of Old Faithful.

1. Our latest budget request perhaps will be approved.

_____

_____

_____

2. The camera obscura, although few people today are familiar with this Renaissance invention, is a predecessor of the modern camera.

_____

_____

_____

3. After the debris was, by the Army Corps of Engineers, cleared, the stream dropped below flood stage.

_____

_____

_____

4. Darwin did not expect his book *The Origin of Species* to as profoundly affect the scientific world as it did.

_____

_____

_____

5. Linotype machines, invented by Otto Mergenthaler and first used by the *New York Tribune* in 1886, can cast a full line of type at a time.

_____

_____

_____

6. People always need to, whenever they plan a trip, make certain the police are notified that they will be away from home.

_____

_____

_____

7. Eating in new restaurants, although it is sometimes a great mistake, is usually quite exciting.

_____

_____

_____

8. Maria, using the money she had earned as a clinical psychologist, bought the stereo equipment she had wanted for several years.

_____

_____

_____

9. Micah watched, through the living-room window, with envy as his older brother and sister left for the first day of school.

_____

_____

_____

10. Nicole hoped, although she had not received any information, to hear about her scholarship in a few days.

_____

_____

_____

11.4 Parallelism

■ *Revise the following sentences to correct faulty parallelism.*

EXAMPLE
Computerized inventory control can save time, insure adequate stock, and is useful in keeping track of sales trends.

Computerized inventory control can save time, insure adequate stock, and help keep track of sales trends.

1. The man was neither for the new taxes or against them.

   _____

   _____

   _____

2. The secretary typed the letters, put stamps on them, and then goes home.

   _____

   _____

   _____

3. Alarmed by the hunters' guns, the ducks rose quickly from the water and were noisy as they flew to safety.

   _____

   _____

   _____

4. The new office building is tall, spacious, and it looks beautiful.

   _____

   _____

   _____

5. Annoyed at the long check-out lines, the shopper began to sigh loudly, tapping his foot, and glance at his watch.

_____

_____

_____

6. Travelers crossing southern Texas pass through Beaumont, Houston, San Antonio, and then they drive to El Paso.

_____

_____

_____

7. The attorney advised her client to testify in his own behalf and against taking the Fifth Amendment.

_____

_____

_____

8. At school he found that he hated eating in the cafeteria, studying for his chemistry class, and laundry.

_____

_____

_____

9. After shopping at the department store, the two friends visited an art gallery and then were watching a movie.

_____

_____

_____

10. Although the fire inside the cabin was warm, the air was damp, the walls were cold, and the wind whispering through the cracks near the windows.

_____

_____

_____

11.5 Parallelism

■ *Revise the following sentences to correct faulty parallelism.*

EXAMPLE

The new decor is in good taste and attractive.

The new decor is tasteful and attractive.

1. The weather reporter predicted rain and that it would not last all day.

   _____

   _____

   _____

2. The timid soul was afraid of dogs, and cats terrified him.

   _____

   _____

   _____

3. Historians study not only the political movements of society but also how the technology changes.

   _____

   _____

   _____

4. The museum either needs some new exhibits or some better tour guides.

   _____

   _____

   _____

5. The Egyptians introduced stone architecture and also are credited with developing the 365-day calendar.

_____

_____

_____

6. To renew one's spirit, to test one's endurance, and feel at peace with nature—these are the benefits of survival hikes.

_____

_____

_____

7. Our vacation will be a success if we visit Carlsbad Caverns, White Sands National Park, and seeing Yellowstone National Park.

_____

_____

_____

8. The contractor opposed the scientists' request that he delay construction and excavating the archaeological site.

_____

_____

_____

9. The Treasury Department scrutinized all the amendments to the tax bills for unintentional loopholes, typographical errors, and to see if they contained windfall tax credits for special interests.

_____

_____

_____

10. Pine trees are the most profitable investment for the forest-products industry; they grow fast, they provide lumber as well as pulp, and naval stores such as turpentines and resins are their by-products.

_____

_____

_____

11.6 Variety in Sentences

■ *Make one sentence out of each of the groups below. Vary your sentences in length, structure, and order. Write simple, compound, and complex patterns, and vary your sentences between loose, periodic, and balanced forms. A loose sentence, the most frequent kind, makes the main point early and then adds refinements. A periodic sentence withholds an element of the main thought until the end and thus creates suspense and emphasis. A balanced sentence has parts that are similar in structure and length and that express parallel thoughts.*

EXAMPLE
The Liberty Bell was rung only twice.
It now sits in Independence Hall.
Independence Hall is in Philadelphia.

The Liberty Bell, which now sits in Independence Hall, Philadelphia, was rung only twice.

1. Chicago's World's Columbian Exposition began in 1893.
   Over 686 acres were lighted by electricity.
   George Washington Ferris introduced the first Ferris wheel.

   _____

   _____

   _____

   _____

2. Mount Everest was named in 1855.
   It was named for Sir George Everest.
   He was a surveyor-general of India.

   _____

   _____

   _____

   _____

3. George Pullman built the first dining car in 1868.
   The car was named *Delmonico*.
   The name of the car came from a famous family of New York City
   restaurateurs.

   _____

   _____

   _____

   _____

4. The Indian kingdom of Quito was in the area that is now called
   Ecuador.
   It was over two thousand years old when the Incas conquered it.
   They conquered it in 1470.

   _____

   _____

   _____

   _____

5. Clothing made of synthetic materials has been popular since World
   War II.
   Cotton is becoming popular again.
   Cotton fabric that will hold a permanent press can now be man-
   ufactured.

   _____

   _____

   _____

   _____

6. The black heartwood of ebony weighs seventy or more pounds per
   cubic foot.
   Persimmon trees are a species of ebony.
   They lack enough black hardwood to make them commercially
   valuable.

   _____

   _____

_____

_____

7. The boisterous children ran toward the cat.
   The cat twitched her tail nervously.
   The cat then sprang away to safety.

   _____

   _____

   _____

   _____

8. The costs of owning a swimming pool are greater than the initial
   construction expenses.
   Pools should be routinely maintained.
   Additional liability insurance is a necessity for the swimming-
   pool owner.

   _____

   _____

   _____

   _____

9. Soft contact lenses are quite popular.
   They require more care than hard contact lenses do.
   The lenses must be washed daily and cleaned with a special
   solution once a month.

   _____

   _____

   _____

   _____

10. Columbus is supposed to have discovered America in the fifteenth
    century.
    Norsemen are credited with discovering the New World about
    A.D. 1000.

The first people to find the New World probably crossed a land
bridge between Siberia and Alaska between 18,000 and 14,000 B.C.

_____

_____

_____

_____

11.7 Variety in Sentences

■ *Revise the following sentences for greatest emphasis and for the most logical or climactic order. Write* **E** *to the left of any effective sentence.*

EXAMPLE

On the legislative agenda are tax reform, billboard regulations, and new committee assignments.

On the legislative agenda are new committee assignments, billboard regulations, and tax reforms.

(Revised to move from least to most important item.)

1. René Descartes retired to write his important philosophical works after serving in the French army for about ten years.

2. An old car frequently fails to start, is uncomfortable, and uses too much oil.

3. The sprinter ran faster than ever before, beat his opponents in the meet, and set a world record.

4. The earthquake destroyed an entire section of the city, interrupted communications, and damaged several highways.

5. The famous novelist toured several countries, won the Nobel Prize, and finished his twentieth book.

_____

_____

6. Drivers prepared themselves for delays, slowed their cars, and turned on their headlights when fog began to cover the Golden Gate Bridge.

_____

_____

_____

7. After the machinist lost her position, she had interviews with several companies, searched the help-wanted advertisements for a new job, and wrote letters listing her qualifications.

_____

_____

_____

8. Both political candidates have previous public service: they have served in the United States Senate, on the state board of mines, and on the local school board.

_____

_____

_____

9. The era of the dirigibles ended when the *Hindenberg* burst into flames above Lakehurst, New Jersey, and killed thirty-six persons.

_____

_____

10. The price of pineapples continued to increase because demand continued to exceed supply.

_____

_____

_____

11.8 Variety in Sentences

■ *Identify the following sentences as loose or periodic.*

EXAMPLES

When wind speeds exceed seventy-five miles an hour, a tropical storm is called a hurricane.

periodic

A tropical storm is called a hurricane when its wind speeds exceed seventy-five miles an hour.

loose

1. After our home was burglarized, we had an alarm system installed. _____

2. Black Friday usually refers to September 19, 1873, when numerous business failures inaugurated the panic of 1873. _____

3. As soon as the new inventory arrived, the stock clerks placed it on the shelves. _____

4. The garage was always messy after her husband worked on his antique Buick. _____

5. Before Clara Barton founded the American Red Cross, she worked as the first woman clerk in the U.S. Patent Office. _____

6. Many of the sailors began to shout when their ship reached landfall and they could see their home port again. _____

7. The group visited the Lincoln Memorial on the last day of their annual visit to Washington. _____

8. Constructed of cedar, brick, and redwood, the new mountain cabins will endure many decades. _____

9. A school-bus driver must undergo special training and purchase a chauffeur's license in order to be hired by any board of education or private school. _____

10. Although most states have laws and regulations that control interest rates, in many instances the laws are either confusing or contradictory. _____

11.9 Variety in Sentences

■ *Make the following loose sentences into periodic ones.*

EXAMPLE

The liver is an irreplaceable organ of the body, for machines cannot duplicate its various and highly complex functions.

Machines cannot duplicate the various and highly complex bodily functions of one irreplaceable organ of the body, the liver.

1. Learning to live with others in the dormitory was difficult for me when I went to college.

   _____

   _____

   _____

2. Charles Dickens's *A Christmas Carol* sold over six thousand copies the first day largely because of its author's popularity.

   _____

   _____

   _____

3. You must follow the directions carefully if you want to avoid making careless errors.

   _____

   _____

   _____

4. I hiked to Big Dry Creek and Little Dry Creek in east-central Montana.

_____

_____

_____

5. Some of the bristlecone pines of California's White Mountains are estimated to be over 4,600 years old although the oldest known redwoods are about 3,500 years old.

_____

_____

_____

6. South Dakota is nicknamed the Sunshine State, though many people prefer to call it the Coyote State.

_____

_____

_____

7. Rodeo champions earn large sums of money each year though not as much as other sports figures receive.

_____

_____

_____

8. The children were surprisingly quiet and attentive during the violinist's solo.

_____

_____

_____

9. Every stamp collector wants a 1928 Graf Zeppelin stamp because it is very rare.

_____

_____

_____

10. The building was finished on the morning before the contract expired.

_____

_____

_____

11.10 Sentence Structure: Review 2

■ *Rewrite the following paragraph to eliminate non-parallel structures as well as dangling and misplaced modifiers.*

The word *Yankee* has an interesting history, but it is of uncertain origin. Some people believe the word came from Europe, where natives of the Netherlands were sometimes called *Jan Kees*; it is the opinion of others that the word is derived from *Anglais*, the French word for English, or perhaps from an Indian pronunciation of the word *English*. Made popular during the Revolutionary War, people of other countries now use the word *Yankee* to refer to any American. Most Americans, though, use the word to refer to New Englanders, while in the states that once belonged to the Confederacy, *Yankee* is used as a term of opprobrium still to refer to anyone who lives in what were the Union states during the American Civil War.

PUNCTUATION

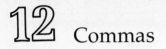 # Commas

USES OF COMMAS

Although commas have many functions, they are used, in general, to separate elements and to set off modifiers or parenthetical elements.

Between Two Independent Clauses

Use the comma to separate independent clauses joined by a coordinating conjunction (*and, but, or, nor, for, so, yet*).

> The brisk winds raised only moderate waves, *but* the falling barometer indicated that stormy weather was coming.

In a Series

Use a comma between words, phrases, and clauses in a series.

> Politicians often address business groups, civic organizations, and schools. (words in a series)
> The audience was seated, the overture had begun, and the curtain was about to open. (clauses in a series)

Between Coordinate Adjectives

Use a comma between **coordinate adjectives** not joined by *and*. Coordinate adjectives each modify the noun (or pronoun) independently.

> The *gloomy, uninhabited* house was very isolated.

Cumulative adjectives do not modify independently. Do not use a comma between cumulative adjectives.

> He discarded his *favorite blue* sweater.

Note: to recognize coordinate adjectives, place the word *and* between them and determine whether they sound right.

> The gloomy *and* uninhabited house was isolated. (sounds right)
> He discarded his favorite *and* blue sweater. (sounds wrong)

Another test is to reverse the adjectives. Normally, coordinate adjectives are easily reversible.

uninhabited, gloomy house (sounds right)

blue favorite sweater (sounds wrong)

After Long Introductory Clauses or Phrases

Use a comma after a long introductory phrase or clause.

> Shortly after the abrupt end of the first act, everyone was certain that the butler had committed the crime. (phrase)
>
> When the first act came to an abrupt end, everyone was certain that the butler had committed the crime. (clause)

An introductory verbal phrase is usually set off by a comma.

> *Working alone*, she built a new room at the mountain retreat. (participial phrase)
>
> *To prepare for the race*, the runner trained for weeks. (infinitive phrase)

With Nonrestrictive Elements

Use commas to set off nonrestrictive appositives, phrases, and clauses that add description or information but are not essential to the meaning of the sentence.

> Geri, the Northside branch manager, expects to be transferred soon. (nonrestrictive appositive phrase)
>
> Geri, who is the Northside branch manager, expects to be transferred soon. (nonrestrictive adjective clause)
>
> Mount Saint Helens, dormant for a long period, erupted with great fury.

Note that a restrictive element is necessary for the meaning of the total sentence and that it is not set off by commas.

> The music *that we most enjoy* is contemporary.

With Conjunctive Adverbs

Use a comma after a conjunctive adverb (*however, nevertheless, moreover, furthermore,* and so on) when it precedes an independent clause.

> The profit margin was down; *however*, next year should be better.

With Sentence Elements Out of Normal Word Order

Use commas with sentence elements out of normal word order.

> The trainer, *haggard and thin*, slowly saddled the horse.

With Degrees, Titles, Dates, Places, Addresses

Use commas with degrees and titles, as well as to separate elements in dates, places, and addresses.

> Rosa Adams, M.D., joined the staff. (comma before and after *M.D.*)
> On March 10, 1971, my daughter was born. (comma before and after year)
> On Monday, December 19, the Christmas vacation begins.
> Sedona, Arizona, is at the entrance to Oak Creek Canyon. (Use a comma before and after the name of a state when the city is named.)

BUT

> In July, 1969, we bought a new home. (optional commas)
> The year 1945 marked the end of World War II. (no comma)
> My new address is 196 Warner Avenue, Westwood, California 73520. (no comma before zip code)

For Contrast or Emphasis

Use commas for contrast and emphasis as well as for short interrogative elements.

> Many doctors believe that exercise, not diet, is the key to weight loss.
> The sheep continued eating, not sensing the cougar's presence.
> You have read this before, haven't you?

With Mild Interjections and *Yes* or *No*

Use commas with mild interjections and with words like *yes* and *no*.

> *Well*, I was almost right.
> *Yes*, we agree to your offer.

With Direct Address

Use commas with words in direct address.

> "Laura, did you receive this letter?"

Use commas with expressions like *he said* or *she replied* when used with quoted matter.

> "I cannot find my raincoat," *he complained*.

With Absolute Phrases

Set off an **absolute phrase** with a comma. An absolute phrase, which consists of a noun followed by a modifier, modifies an entire sentence.

> *The restaurant being closed,* we decided to go home.

To Prevent Misreading or to Mark an Omission

Use commas to prevent misreading or to mark an omission.

> Above, the wind howled through the trees.
>
> The summer days were hot and dry; the nights, warm and humid. (comma for omitted verb *were*)

12.1 Commas with Independent Clauses

■ *In the following sentences, insert and circle commas between independent clauses. In the blank at the right, enter the comma and the coordinating conjunction. If a sentence is correct, write* **C**.

EXAMPLE

The wheel of fortune was a significant symbol in many ancient cultures⊚and it appears in the works of both Dante and Chaucer.   ___, *and*___

1. About one-third of the passengers on the *May-flower* left England for religious reasons and the other two-thirds were adventurers.   _____

2. The nuclear power industry claims that atomic plants have been criticized unfairly but many scientists believe that the problems are even greater than originally thought.   _____

3. The numerals we use today are commonly known as Arabic numerals but were actually invented by the people of India and are sometimes called Hindu numerals.   _____

4. The Labrador retriever sat in the back of the pickup truck and it seemed to enjoy the wind blowing in its face.   _____

5. The marketing survey we conducted before production started only confirmed the project manager's intuitions.   _____

6. The value of an entire coin collection depends on the worth of a few rare pieces and on the condition of all the coins in a set. _____

7. More than twenty-seven million acres of Alaska belong to national forests, parks, and monuments, but the best known is probably Mount McKinley National Park. _____

8. The company's comptroller personally approved all vouchers for travel expenses and warned all employees against overspending. _____

9. The diver realized the danger in attempting a new record height in the brisk wind but he asked the judges for permission to raise the platform. _____

10. Many restaurants in New England are famous for their seafood and some also have fine views of the Atlantic Ocean and the fishing boats of coastal waters. _____

12.2 Commas with Independent Clauses

■ *In the following sentences, insert and circle commas between independent clauses. In the blank at the right, enter the comma and the coordinating conjunction. If a sentence is correct, write* **C**.

EXAMPLES

Polls are not always reliable‚but most companies still use them.

_____, but_____

The use of alcohol as automotive fuel is hardly a new idea‚ for Henry Ford designed the Model T to use it.

_____, for_____

1. Archaeologists have uncovered many interesting artifacts near Tallahassee, Florida, and now they better understand Indian life at the time of De-Soto's first encounter with native Americans.

_____

2. Many experts in the late 1970s thought the widespread use of computers would reduce the need for accountants but those predictions have been proven incorrect.

_____

3. Many students seek part-time employment during their vacations so unemployment rates rise during the summer months.

_____

4. Lady Astor was the wife of Waldorf Astor and the first woman member of the British House of Commons.

_____

5. Many of the books in the library were very old and the librarian knew there was little money available to save them.

_____

6. The docks were empty when the ship began to approach but suddenly they came alive with workers ready to unload the cargo. _____

7. The small painting being auctioned was by a relatively minor sixteenth-century artist but it was valued at almost a quarter of a million dollars. _____

8. The city's Parks and Recreation Department has started evening crafts classes for adults, and they are attracting many people. _____

9. Dr. Cagnilia kicked her golf ball out of the sand trap, but her playing partner caught her cheating. _____

10. Infrared photographs of the earth's geography help to determine the extent of droughts and they also are invaluable aids in the search for mineral deposits. _____

12.3 Commas with Items in a Series

■ *Insert and circle commas as necessary in items in a series.*

EXAMPLE

Charities solicit funds from businesses⊙civic groups⊙and individuals.

1. The Pleiades Taurus and Orion are three of the best-known winter constellations in the Northern Hemisphere.

2. American English continually drops old words adds new ones and develops new connotations for familiar expressions.

3. The cat's eyes glared intensely its tail twitched nervously and its hair rose instinctively as it watched the approaching dog.

4. Many recreational vehicles have complete kitchens that include compact refrigerators ranges and sinks.

5. The participants in the decathlon had completed all the events but the javelin throw the broad jump and the mile run.

6. Many small businesses use microcomputers for tracking inventory billing customers and figuring monthly payrolls.

7. "We have itemized deductions computed our refund and signed our tax returns," sighed the weary husband.

8. We gave our dog away because in one day it had bitten the mail carrier run our neighbor's cat up a tree and chased a delivery truck.

9. Birds eat harmful insects scatter seeds and spread pollen; thus they serve a variety of ecological functions.

10. When my grandfather was young, he went to the movies on Saturday morning and watched several cartoons a serial and two full-length films for a mere quarter.

12.4 Commas with Coordinate Adjectives

■ *Insert and circle commas as necessary between coordinate adjectives.*

EXAMPLE

The garden court is a new‿exciting concept in motel design.

1. The small group was engaged in a quiet desultory conversation.

2. The bright cheerful greeting made me feel welcome.

3. The small hardy Lapps speak a language related to Finnish.

4. Many corporations are looking for employees with sound liberal arts backgrounds as well as aggressive entrepreneurial personalities.

5. The carpenter worked long hard hours on the new room.

6. The traffic study showed that many automobiles were using the new well-designed bypass.

7. Many people now enjoy sturdy inexpensive trampolines in their yards.

8. The student of interior design must learn the modern energy-efficient ways of accent lighting.

9. Few Americans are familiar with the sharp piercing cry of the coyote.

10. "Laughter, I believe, is the best least expensive medicine," said the speaker.

12.5 Commas After Introductory Clauses or Phrases

■ *Place and circle commas as needed after introductory clauses or phrases. In the space at the right, place the comma and write the word after it. If a sentence is punctuated correctly or requires no punctuation, write C.*

EXAMPLE
When mortgage rates are high realtors seek alternatives to conventional financing.
                                                                    , realtors

1. Built in 1769 and used to pull French artillery the world's first automobile, a steam carriage, was built by Captain Nicolas Cugnot. _____

2. Although Michael enjoyed playing in the orchestra he did not like practicing. _____

3. After discovering the relation between bacteria and infection Joseph Lister revolutionized medicine by developing antiseptic surgical procedures. _____

4. Because the storm had torn down the power lines the family had to spend the night in a motel. _____

5. After Linda's engagement ring had been sized she showed it to her friends. _____

6. How frustrated candidates control themselves and their ardent followers in defeat may determine their chances for future political races. _____

7. Covering more than 650,000 square miles the Great Artesian Basin is an important underground source of water in eastern Australia. _____

8. For lunch many workers drink coffee, eat a package of cheese crackers, and then return to work. _____

9. Although citizens-band radios are not as powerful as short-wave sets they nevertheless furnish hours of enjoyment to many motorists. _____

10. "Whatever we do this Saturday," Victor said, "I want to be home in time for the wrestling program on television." _____

12.6 Commas After Introductory Clauses or Phrases

■ *Place and circle commas as needed after introductory clauses or phrases. In the space provided at the right, place the comma and write the word after it. If a sentence is punctuated correctly or requires no punctuation, write **C**.*

EXAMPLE

Although most engineers are college graduates⊙they may
need continual technical training.   *,they*

1. After the demise of vaudeville many of its stars became radio and television entertainers. _____

2. Although the word *hound* once referred to any kind of dog it now chiefly refers to certain types of hunting dogs. _____

3. Even though the meeting was considered a success many in the group felt much of the work remained unfinished. _____

4. Almost twice the size of the United States Siberia contains only one-sixth as many people. _____

5. Stepping into her limousine the diplomat suddenly turned and waved to the crowd. _____

6. Since 1924 winter sports have been included in the Olympic Games. _____

7. Because of requests from doctors, parents, and students physical hygiene is being taught in many public schools. _____

8. Although most of Mars's visible water now appears as polar ice and atmospheric vapor water may have flowed in rivers on the Martian surface thousands of years ago. _____

9. To escape the crowd some people leave a few minutes before ball games are over. _____

10. Until my ship actually sailed for the Far East, I never imagined that I would ever have the opportunity to see Japan. _____

12.7 Commas with Nonrestrictive Elements

■ *Correctly punctuate nonrestrictive elements in the following sentences. Write C to the right of any correctly punctuated sentence. Circle punctuation that you add.*

EXAMPLE

Janice‚who is our first choice for the position‚has accepted a job with another company.

1. Giuseppe Verdi's *Aida* first produced in 1871 is still one of the world's most popular operas. _____

2. Optometrists who are allowed to prescribe glasses are not allowed to use surgery or drugs to treat their patients. _____

3. Ornate weather vanes which once topped most American homes are again becoming popular. _____

4. The letter that I wrote today should be in Portland by Thursday. _____

5. Many companies that were founded as private firms have recently sold public stock. _____

6. The oak tree that is outside my bedroom window is almost as tall as our two-story house. _____

7. Blueberries which may be cultivated in large fields make splendid jellies and jams. _____

8. The new municipal airport which opened last week is several miles from the city. _____

9. Professional counseling in elementary school which is a relatively new field can make a dramatic difference in the scholastic performance of young children. _____

10. John Richardson who is the chef at my father's restaurant does not like to prepare food for large groups. _____

12.8 Commas—All Uses

■ *Correctly punctuate the following sentences. Circle punctuation that you add.*

EXAMPLE

Denver, Colorado, and San Diego, California, are two of the most rapidly growing cities in the United States.

1. The meeting scheduled for Tuesday January 15 has been postponed until Thursday January 24.

2. Alicia McMurray C.P.A. was employed by the firm of Feldman Parsons and Ames.

3. Sequoia National Park established on September 25 1890 is the nation's second oldest national park.

4. Most of the works of Phidias Myron and Praxiteles three of the great sculptors of classical Greece have been lost or destroyed.

5. The international Morse code a form of the original Morse code used in international telegraphy is sometimes called the continental code.

6. Whenever we hear that snow has fallen in the nearby mountains we pack up the car and spend the weekend there.

7. The American Council of Learned Societies located at 345 East 46th Street New York New York 10017 sponsors many kinds of fellowships in various academic disciplines.

8. On this date October 12 1984 the small collection of houses called Arno New Mexico was formally incorporated and it installed its first mayor city council and school board.

9. "Although it is a relatively small city Bismarck North Dakota is the state capital and is twice as large as Pierre South Dakota which is also a state capital" stated the visiting lecturer in Geography 101.

10. Sandra Day O'Connor a jurist from Arizona was the first woman appointed to the United States Supreme Court.

12.9 Commas—All Uses

■ *Correctly punctuate the following sentences. Circle punctuation that you add. Write* **C** *in the blank at the right if the sentence is correct.*

EXAMPLE

A good speaker⊙using an occasional pause⊙allows an audi-

ence a chance to respond. _____

1. Heinrich Schliemann the discoverer of ancient

   Troy became an American citizen in 1850. _____

2. Any citizen of the United States may communi-

   cate with the President simply by addressing a

   letter to 1600 Pennsylvania Avenue Washington

   DC 20500. _____

3. However eager good salespersons may be to com-

   plete a sale they will never appear impatient. _____

4. "The Sanscrit word *mata*" the linguist assured us

   "is related to the English word *mother*." _____

5. To settle legal disputes among themselves many

   nations turn to the International Court of Justice

   the main judicial body of the United Nations. _____

6. We finally could not resist playing a practical joke

   on Raymond because he had played so many

   on us. _____

7. The eager industrious volunteers worked to com-

   plete the homecoming float. _____

8. Lifting the antique glass to the light to examine its color, examining the engraving and lightly tapping its sides the expert judged it to be highly valuable.   _____

9. To a shaggy long-haired dog that can find little relief from the summer heat a cool bare concrete floor is a great blessing.   _____

10. On January 18 1989 Charles Richardson an active man throughout his life celebrated his eighty-seventh birthday.   _____

12.10 Commas: Review

■ *Revise the following paragraph to correct all errors in the use of commas.*

Samuel Johnson one of England's most colorful men of letters lived a life filled with contradictions. He was a scholarly man fluent in Greek Latin and French but he welcomed many poor uneducated people into his household. Although a deeply religious man he frequently suffered from religious doubts. He had a reputation for sloth yet he almost single-handedly compiled the first comprehensive English dictionary a remarkable feat when one considers that he was nearly blind as a result of a childhood case of scrofula. Although his contemporaries knew him as a poet an essayist and a brilliant conversationalist he is perhaps best remembered today as a lexicographer.

Unnecessary Commas

Do not use commas excessively. Placing commas at all pauses in sentences is not a correct practice.

Between Subject and Verb

Do not use a comma between subject and verb, between verb or verbal and complement, or between an adjective and the word it modifies.

NOT

> The team with the best record, will go to the playoffs.
>
> We saw, that the window had been left open.
>
> The shining wrapping, paper caught one's attention. (Delete commas.)

Between Compound Elements

Do not use a comma between compound elements, such as verbs, subjects, complements, and predicates.

NOT

> We went to the local library, and perused *The New York Times*. (Delete comma.)

Between Dependent Clauses

Do not use a comma before a coordinating conjunction joining two dependent clauses.

NOT

> We checked to see that the lights were off, and that all the doors were locked. (Delete comma.)

In Comparisons

Do not use a comma before *than* in a comparison or between compound conjunctions such as *as . . . as, so . . . so, so . . . that*.

NOT

> The electrician found more wrong with the washing machine, than we had expected.
>
> It was so hot, that the engine overheated. (Delete commas.)

After *Like, Such As*

Do not use a comma after *like* or *such as*. A comma is used before *such as* only when the phrase is nonrestrictive.

Many famous paintings such as, the *Mona Lisa* and *View of Toledo* are almost priceless. (Delete comma.)

Do not use a comma directly before or after a period, a question mark, an exclamation point, or a dash.

"Were you late for work?", he asked. (Delete comma.)

With Parentheses

A comma may follow a closing parenthesis but may not come before an opening parenthesis.

After reading *The Color Purple* (written by Alice Walker), one better understands the cultural roots of black Americans.

Other Unnecessary Commas

Do not use commas after coordinating conjunctions.

We did not like the accommodations at the hotel, but, we found nothing else available. (Retain comma before *but*; delete comma after *but*.)

A comma is not required after short adverbial modifiers.

After a rain the desert blooms with wildflowers. (no comma required after *rain*)

Do not use commas to set off restrictive clauses, phrases, or appositives.

The water level, *at the lake*, is low. (restrictive prepositional phrase)

Do not use a comma between adjectives that are cumulative and not coordinate. (See p. 176)

The new, Persian rug was beautiful.

13.1 Unnecessary Commas

■ *Circle all unnecessary commas in the following sentences.*

EXAMPLE

People who live in glass houses should not throw stones.

1. The ribbed vault, the flying buttress, and the pointed arch, characterize Gothic architecture.

2. The ferocious, black hornet is really a member of the wasp family, and, is, believe it or not, a very social insect.

3. The dingo, a wolf-like, wild, dog of Australia, is a natural enemy of sheep herds.

4. Asphalt is one of many valuable petroleum by-products, that have helped transform modern society.

5. Aberrations in Neptune's orbit, led to careful astronomical observations that confirmed the existence, of the planet Pluto.

6. Of some botanical interest, is a plant called, rattlesnake root, which has tubers that supposedly cure rattlesnake bites—, at least many early settlers thought so.

7. The famous, Oregon Trail covered two thousand miles of frontier from Independence, Missouri, to Portland, Oregon, and it was heavily traveled, during the westward migrations of the nineteenth century.

8. The unusually, careful driver ahead of us slowed everyone in our lane.

9. One of the shells, that we found at the beach turned out to be valuable.

10. The last of the South American artifacts, shown at the museum, were packed, and prepared for shipping at the end of the week.

13.2 Unnecessary Commas

■ *Circle all unnecessary commas in the following sentences.*

EXAMPLE
I am sure that the investment‿was a wise one.

1. An effective résumé includes a summary of a job applicant's major skills, as well as a précis of his or her education, and work experiences.

2. Over twenty-nine million copies, of *The Official Boy Scout Handbook*, have been sold, since its first edition was published in 1910.

3. Of all the poems I have read recently, Thomas Hardy's lyric, "The Darkling Thrush," and Alfred, Lord Tennyson's, *In Memoriam*, seem the most pertinent to our times.

4. The shadow of the massive, ageless, oak fell upon the young, and carefree lovers, as they planned with infinite faith, for the future.

5. So great was the influence of Thomas Paine, on his own time, that John Adams suggested, that the era be called, "The Age of Paine."

6. One should never be ashamed, however, of being somewhat emotional, for, a certain amount of emotion, can help keep a person warm and human.

7. By 1910, some demographers predicted, that the population of Western Europe would begin to decline, and that, by the end of the century, Eastern Europe would be more populous than Western Europe.

8. Migrant, fur traders played an important role in the exploration of the American West.

9. Our new piano will be delivered this week, possibly, by Wednesday.

10. The Coast Guard launch, skipped across the water, quickly slowed, and then turned, toward the pier.

14 Semicolons, Colons, Dashes, Parentheses, and Brackets

SEMICOLONS

Between Two Independent Clauses

Use a semicolon between independent clauses not joined by *and, but, or, nor, for, so,* or *yet.*

> In the 1950s, manned space flight was only a dream; in the 1960s, it was a reality.

Use a semicolon before a conjunctive adverb that introduces an independent clause.

> Meredith and I removed the defective part; then we sent a letter of complaint to the manufacturer.

Use a semicolon to separate independent clauses that are long and complex or that have internal punctuation.

> Central City, located near Denver, was once a mining town in the nineteenth century; but since the decline of the mining industry, it has become noted for its summer opera program.

Between Items in a Series

Use semicolons in a series between items that have internal punctuation (usually commas).

> In his closet Bill kept a photograph album, which was empty; several tennis shoes, all with holes in them; and the radiator cap from his first car, which he sold his first year in college.

Do not use a semicolon between elements that are not coordinate.

INCORRECT
> After publishing *The Day of the Jackal* and several other popular novels; Frederick Forsyth wrote his most exciting book, *The Devil's Alternative.* (Use a comma, not a semicolon.)

COLONS

Use a colon before quotations, statements, and series that are introduced formally.

The geologist began his speech with a disturbing statement: "This country is short of rare metals."

Use a colon to introduce a formal series.

> Bring the following items to the test: lined paper, two pencils, and a calculator.

Between Two Independent Clauses

Use a colon between two independent clauses when the second explains the first.

> Some car buyers base their decisions on a single criterion: does the dealership have a reputation for giving good service?

For Special Uses

Use the colon between hours and minutes.

> 4:35 P.M.

Unnecessary Colon

Do not use a colon *after* a linking verb or a preposition.

INCORRECT

> Our best sales representatives are: Steven Walsh and Maria Moreno.
>
> Ron asked us to: list the items we needed, explain their use, and estimate their cost.

DASHES

Use dashes to introduce summaries or to show interruption, parenthetical comment, or special emphasis.

For Summary

> Clothing, blankets, food, medicine—anything will help.

For Interruption

> Seven of my colleagues—I can't recall their names now—signed the petition.

For Parenthetical Comments

> This is important—I mean really important—so listen carefully.

For Special Emphasis

The key to the mystery could be in only one place—the attic.

PARENTHESES

Use parentheses to enclose loosely related comments or explanations or to enclose numbers used to indicate items in a series.

That year (1950) was the happiest time of my life.

Please do the following: (1) fill out the form, (2) include a check or money order, and (3) list any special mailing instructions.

BRACKETS

Use brackets to enclose *interpolations*—that is, the writer's explanations—within a passage that is being quoted.

The senator objected: "I cannot agree with your [Senator Miner's] reasoning." (brackets used to set off writer's interpolation)

14.1 Semicolons

■ *Insert semicolons where they are needed in the following sentences. If necessary, cross out other marks of punctuation. Circle semicolons that you add.*

EXAMPLE

Tropical rain forests are incredibly luxuriant; they are, however, disappearing rapidly.

1. In 1900 the average life expectancy for an American was 47.3 years, by 1975 this average had increased to 72.4 years.

2. Some railroads use simulated locomotives to train engineers others depend on the traditional apprenticeship system.

3. The Domesday Book is the oldest public record in Britain it was commissioned by William the Conqueror and completed in 1086.

4. Australia's Bicentennial gift to the United States was an endowed chair in Australian studies at Harvard University, another gift was a copy of the Magna Carta from Great Britain.

5. A group of whales is known as a *gam* a group of toads is called a *knot*.

6. Scientific prediction of earthquakes remains primitive and haphazard, nevertheless, scientists can make general predictions after monitoring magnetic charges along major faults.

7. Automatic transmission and air conditioning account for higher automotive fuel costs: for a luxury, eight-cylinder car the additional cost per ten thousand miles may reach $350, for a compact car, $150, and for a six-cylinder subcompact, $200.

8. Scientists say that brain research offers the promise of treating many serious diseases others claim that scientists may be exploring areas best left untouched.

9. Many coastal communities first met the threat of beach erosion with sea walls then they resorted to replacing the sand that had washed away.

10. For years aircraft designers have attempted to reduce the weight of planes by using lighter metals now they are using reinforced light-weight materials that virtually eliminate most of the metal formerly used.

14.2 Semicolons

■ *Insert semicolons where they are needed in the following sentences. If necessary, cross out other marks of punctuation. Circle semicolons that you add.*

EXAMPLE

The project was time-consuming; it lasted a week longer than scheduled.

1. The city manager proposed a graduated income tax, the council preferred a sales tax to increase revenues.

2. To the early Mormon settlers, the Colorado Plateau was unattractive, to later pioneers, it was a pastoral vista of tranquility and color.

3. In 1982, nearly 2,000 newspapers employed about 40,000 reporters that year, magazines hired approximately 120,000 writers and editors.

4. Epoxy glue can join together almost any kind of material except rubber and some plastics, indeed, the bond of the glue is often stronger than the original material.

5. Prospective pet owners should investigate thoroughly what kinds of animals best fit their lifestyles then the pets they choose may be pleasures rather than nuisances to them.

6. When purchasing an automobile battery, the consumer should compare various brands and sizes, standards of comparison may include a battery's cold-cranking power, reserve capacity, ampere-hour capacity, and total number of plates.

7. The most highly paid butlers, whose annual salaries exceed $50,000, are knowledgeable about food, wine, and formal etiquette capable

of managing and supervising large household staffs and gifted with discreet, diplomatic temperaments.

8. The United States is the only nation besides Burma that has not officially begun converting to the metric system, however, an estimated one-fourth of U.S. manufacturers now use metric measurement.

9. Some people's lives are driven by desperation others' lives are guided by inspiration.

10. At present NASA is choosing the basic design of the first permanent United States space station as early as the mid-1990s, the first sections of the orbiter may be in place.

14.3 Colons and Dashes

■ *Correctly punctuate the following sentences. Circle punctuation that you add. Write C to the left of any sentence that is correct.*

EXAMPLE

All of New England⊖Connecticut, Maine, Massachusetts, New Hampshire, Rhode Island, and Vermont⊖is likely to suffer serious fuel shortages during bad winters.

1. The first speaker described one phenomenon jogging that she believes reflects many contemporary values of society.

2. Many theaters find that an 815 curtain time means fewer latecomers than one at 800.

3. The cotton gin invented by a man from Massachusetts on a visit to Georgia helped to shape the economic destinies of both North and South.

4. A good bird watcher makes identifications using the following characteristics voice, color, size, type of bill, markings, and range.

5. The number of personal computers in public schools skyrocketed in the early 1980s it climbed from 31,000 in 1981 to 630,000 in 1984.

6. Ragweed, mesquite, pine all produce common allergies.

7. The most common means of evaluation the intelligence test is no longer considered sufficient as the sole criterion for placement in special classes.

8. The demand for some construction workers carpenters, electricians, and plumbers is expected to continue rising through the 1990s.

9. After the FAA completed its examination of the wreckage, it concluded that there could be only one reason for the crash pilot error.

10. Halfway down the page the following admonition appeared in bold print DO NOT WRITE BELOW THIS LINE.

14.4 Parentheses and Brackets

■ *Insert parentheses and brackets where they are needed in the following sentences. Circle parentheses and brackets that you add.*

EXAMPLE
One type of blueberry (the rabbit-eye) is native to the Deep South.

1. The administration of Franklin D. Roosevelt 1932–1945 was the longest of any president.

2. Saint Valentine's Day February 14 is observed in honor of a Christian martyr.

3. The Asian elephant's gestation period 645 days is longer than any other animal's.

4. The agronomist considered soybeans the crop of the future because 1 they are hearty; 2 they are high in protein; and 3 they require relatively little expensive fertilizer.

5. Descriptions may be *objective* focusing on the object itself or *subjective* focusing on an individual's response to the object.

6. The expert on etiquette she had written four books on the subject concluded: "Good manners reveal it good breeding; therefore, one should take it seriously."

7. Many physicians believe that most people would enjoy good health if they would a eat modestly, b exercise regularly, and c maintain an optimistic attitude.

8. Before going on a vacation, people should 1 stop all deliveries, 2 ask a neighbor to watch their house, and 3 make certain that all doors and windows are locked.

9. Some options for savers mutual funds, tax-exempt bonds, and zero-coupon bonds are imperfectly understood by many consumers.

10. "That was the year 1965," he said, "when we planned to expand our market to include the West Coast."

Quotation Marks and
End Punctuation

QUOTATION MARKS

Use quotation marks to enclose the exact words of a speaker or writer.

> "I'm glad you came," she said. (declarative statement and object of verb *said*)
>
> "Turn in your papers," he demanded. (command)
>
> "Have you already finished?" she asked. (question)
>
> "Look out!" he cried. (exclamation)

Periods and *commas* always are placed inside quotation marks. *Semicolons* and *colons* always are placed outside quotation marks. *Question marks* and *exclamation points* are placed inside quotation marks when they refer to the quotation itself. They are placed outside the quotation marks when they refer to the entire sentence.

> Who said, "We need a new car"? (Quotation is a statement.)

Use quotation marks to enclose dialogue. Do not use quotation marks with indirect quotations.

> Alexander Pope once wrote, "A little learning is a dangerous thing." (direct quotation)
>
> Alexander Pope said that a little learning can be dangerous. (indirect quotation)

In dialogue a new paragraph marks each change of speaker.

> "Do you have change for a dollar?" the customer asked, after searching in his pocket for change.
> "I think so," replied the cashier.

Quotation Within a Quotation

Use single quotation marks to enclose a quotation within a quotation.

> "I do not know what you mean when you say, 'Improve your extension,'" complained the novice skater.

Titles

Use quotation marks to enclose the titles of essays, articles, short stories, chapters, television programs that are not serials, and short musical compositions.

> We enjoy reading William Safire's column, "On Language," in the Sunday newspaper. (article in newspaper)
>
> The band began to play Sousa's "Stars and Stripes Forever." (musical composition)

Unnecessary Quotation Marks

Do not use quotation marks to emphasize or change the usual meanings of words or to point out the use of slang or attempts at humor. If you must use such language, let it stand without comment.

INCORRECT

> We had a "great" time at the party. (emphasis)
>
> That movie was really "bad." (change of meaning)
>
> I guess we "goofed." (slang)
>
> His lemonades are so bad that they always turn out to be "lemons." (attempted humor)

END PUNCTUATION

Use a period after sentences that make statements and after sentences that express a command that is not exclamatory.

> The restaurant is crowded. (statement)
>
> Call me in the morning. (mild command)

Use a question mark after a direct question.

> How long have you been waiting?

Use an exclamation point after a word, a phrase, or a sentence to indicate strong feeling.

> Ouch! That hurt!
>
> Stop that man!

Remember to use a period after mild exclamations.

> That is the craziest idea I ever heard.

15.1 Quotation Marks and End Punctuation

■ *Correctly punctuate the following sentences. Circle any incorrect punctuation and indicate what punctuation should be used. Indicate a new paragraph with the sign ¶.*

EXAMPLE

"Where do we keep these files?" asked the manager ¶ With the Smith account," replied her secretary.

1. Where was Patrick Henry when he said Give me liberty or give me death?

2. What number are you trying to call? the operator asked politely.

3. Keep your bicycle in top condition for safe riding advised the instruction booklet.

4. What sort of experience leads a young person to choose the life of a surgeon inquired the patient.

5. The social scientist summarized as follows: Because young people generally have values in opposition to those of adult society, youth can be classified as a genuine subculture.

6. An increase in radon in well water said the science reporter may become a means for geologists to predict earthquakes.

7. So many foreign visitors were anticipated by Greek officials that they made arrangements for several ships to provide accommodations for tourists without hotel reservations explained the travel agent.

8. No student will leave my class, announced the English professor, without reading Flannery O'Connor's short story A Good Man Is Hard to Find.

9. The press corps asked exactly what the role of the President's science adviser would be?

10. Did you know that some of the officers in the American Revolution came to this country from Poland specifically to help us win the war asked the history instructor. Our town, Pulaski, Tennessee, is named for one of them a student answered. Correct that was Count Casimir Pulaski responded the teacher.

15.2 Quotation Marks and End Punctuation

■ *Correctly punctuate the following sentences. Circle any incorrect punctuation. Indicate a new paragraph with the sign ¶.*

EXAMPLE
The referee's cry (Stop! You are out of bounds) was lost in the noise of the crowd.

1. The article's title, The Ethics of Price Fixing, is sure to stimulate response.

2. To freeze peaches droned the television chef use citric acid to prevent the fruit from turning brown.

3. Although considered "strange" by his friends, Raymond was actually only very shy.

4. "Why do I have to go to the dentist," the child asked?

5. "Who said, "The only place that he would be the life of the party is in a mortuary?"

6. Listen! whispered the bird watcher, I hear the call of a Baltimore oriole.

7. When my daughter completes her B.S. continued the proud father she expects to begin work toward her M.S. and eventually to earn her Ph.D.

8. Do you remember the name of the man who wrote To Helen asked the librarian.

9. "None of the current methods of increasing the energy supply of America appears to be adequate", writes Wilson Clark in "It Takes Energy to Get Energy".

10. Can you come by the house today? Mary asked. No, I haven't the time, Craig answered. But I can come tomorrow. Fine, I'll see you then.

MECHANICS

16 Underlining for Italics

Underline titles of books (except the Bible and its divisions), periodicals, newspapers, motion pictures, long musical compositions (operas and symphonies, for example), works of art, plays, and works published separately, and occasionally, words to be emphasized.

TITLES

Books

The World Almanac

Periodicals

U.S. News & World Report

Newspapers

Washington Post or the Washington Post

Motion Pictures

Psycho

Musical Compositions, Paintings, and Sculpture

Handel's Messiah
Rodin's The Thinker

Plays

Hamlet

NAMES OF SHIPS AND TRAINS

Underline the names of ships and trains.

The U.S.S. Nimitz
the Zephyr

FOREIGN WORDS

Underline foreign words used in an English context if they have not become a part of our language. Check the dictionary before underlining foreign words.

The policy of <u>glasnost</u>, or open discussion, has brought about some significant changes in the Soviet Union.

WORDS BEING NAMED

Underline words, letters, and figures being named.

The word <u>effigy</u> comes from the Latin term for image.

Be sure to cross your <u>t</u>'s.

FOR OCCASIONAL EMPHASIS

Although underlining for emphasis is permissible on occasion, avoid excessive underlining because it often reveals a writer's weak vocabulary.

NOT

That is not just a big dinner. That is a <u>big</u> dinner.

IMPROVED

That is not just a big dinner. That is a feast.

16.1 Italics

■ *Underline for italics in the following sentences.*

EXAMPLE
<u>The Verdict</u> is a superb movie about modern journalism.

1. Unlike other newspapers, USA Today is distributed nationwide.

2. Lorry is the British word for truck.

3. People learning to pronounce English as a foreign language often find l's, g's, and k's to be troublesome.

4. The Union ironclad Monitor is generally considered the forerunner of the modern warship.

5. Millions of tourists see Charles Lindbergh's aircraft, the Spirit of St. Louis, at the Smithsonian Institution.

6. The common abbreviation A.M. stands for ante meridiem, a Latin phrase meaning "before noon."

7. The United States Navy recommissioned the U.S.S. New Jersey, a World War II battleship.

8. William Least Heat Moon's journal Blue Highways appeared in 1982.

9. Peter and the Wolf is a musical composition written especially for children.

10. The New York Times publishes multiple editions daily for distribution throughout the nation.

16.2 Italics

■ *Underline for italics in the following sentences.*

EXAMPLE
<u>Audubon: A Vision</u> is a long poem by Robert Penn Warren.

1. The United States, not the Queen Elizabeth II, was the largest ocean liner ever built.

2. Roger Tory Peterson's A Field Guide to the Birds has been called the most authoritative book for bird watchers.

3. Peter Shaffer's Amadeus was well received as both a play and a film.

4. The word urbane has been used to describe magazines such as National Geographic and Discover.

5. Agatha Christie's The Mousetrap holds the record as the longest-running play.

6. A roman à clef is a novel that, like Thomas Wolfe's Look Homeward, Angel, presents real people and events under fictional guises.

7. Smithsonian magazine features articles on a wide range of topics.

8. Vivaldi's Four Seasons is a masterpiece of baroque music.

9. The Seventh Seal and Wild Strawberries are two of Ingmar Bergman's better-known films.

10. The Washington Post is the only newspaper published in Washington, D.C.

17 Spelling

Spell correctly. Use a dictionary when you are uncertain of the spelling of a word.

Be particularly careful with words that are not spelled as they sound (*though* and *debt*), words that sound the same (*sew* and *so*), words with the "uh" sound, which gives no clue to their spelling (*terrible* and *persistent*).

Do not misspell words by omitting a syllable that is occasionally and erroneously not pronounced (*accidently* for *accidentally*), by adding syllables (*mischievious* for *mischievous*), or by changing syllables (*preform* for *perform*).

GUIDES FOR SPELLING

For *ie* and *ei*

Use *i* before *e* (*believe*) except after *c* (*receive*) or when these letters are sounded as *a* (*neighbor*). There are a few exceptions (*either, neither, leisure, seize, weird, height*).

Final *e*

Drop the final *e* when adding a **suffix** if the suffix begins with a vowel (*dine* to *dining*). Keep the *e* if the suffix begins with a consonant (*improve* to *improvement*). There are some exceptions (for example, *judge* becomes *judgment*, *notice* becomes *noticeable*, and *awe* becomes *awful*).

For Changing *y* to *i*

Change the *y* to *i* when the *y* is preceded by a consonant, but not when the *y* is preceded by a vowel or when *-ing* is added (*story* becomes *stories*, *delay* becomes *delays*, and *fly* becomes *flying*).

Suffixes

If a suffix begins with a consonant, do not double the final consonant of a word (*quick* becomes *quickly*). If the suffix begins with a vowel, double the last consonant of one-syllable words (*bat* becomes *batting*) and of words of more than one syllable if the accent is on the last syllable (*occur'* becomes *occurrence*). Do not double the final consonant if that consonant is preceded by two vowels (*repair* becomes *repairing*), or if the word ends with two or more consonants (*drink* becomes *drinking*), or if the last syllable of the word is not stressed after the suffix is added (*prefer'* becomes *pref'erence*).

233

Plurals

Add -s for plurals of most nouns (*sound* becomes *sounds*) and for nouns ending in *o* when it is preceded by a vowel (*portfolio* becomes *portfolios*). Add -es when the plural has another syllable that is pronounced (*speech* becomes *speeches*) and in most cases when the noun ends in *o* preceded by a consonant (*tomato* becomes *tomatoes*). See a dictionary for the exceptions.

The plurals of proper names are generally formed by adding -s or -es (*Taylor, Taylors; Jones, Joneses*).

17.1 Suffixes

■ *In the blank spaces provided, write the correct spellings of the following words.*

EXAMPLE

cite / ing _____ *citing* _____

1. compel / ing _____

2. equip / ing _____

3. note / able _____

4. notice / able _____

5. permit / ed _____

6. forbid / en _____

7. write / ing _____

8. use / age _____

9. eat / able _____

10. real / istic _____

11. full / ness _____

12. like / able _____

13. become / ing _____

14. interchange / able _____

15. breathe / ing _____

16. beauty / eous _____

17. commit / ing _____

18. reverse / ible _____

19. defy / ance _____

20. occur / ing _____

21. fry / ed _____

22. fry / ing _____

23. lose / ing _____

24. recur / ed _____

25. cancel / ed _____

17.2 Suffixes

■ *In the blank spaces provided, write the correct spellings of the following words.*

EXAMPLE

stop / ing _____ *stopping* _____

1. carry / er _____

2. believe / able _____

3. tardy / ness _____

4. possible / ity _____

5. compassion / ate _____

6. dine / ing _____

7. true / ly _____

8. lone / liness _____

9. conceive / able _____

10. envy / able _____

11. net / ing _____

12. omit / ed _____

13. accrue / ing _____

14. prescribe / ing _____

15. admit / ance _____

16. marvel / ous _____

17. travel / ed _____

18. adequate / ly _____

19. courage / ous _____

20. practice / able _____

21. retrieve / able _____

22. achieve / ment _____

23. severe / ly _____

24. guarantee / ing _____

25. ninety / eth _____

17.3 Spelling with *ie* and *ei*

■ *Fill in the blanks in the following words with* **ie** *or* **ei***.*

EXAMPLE

defic__*ie*__nt

1. consc_____nce

2. rel_____ve

3. conc_____t

4. w_____ght

5. forf_____t

6. p_____r

7. financ_____r

8. gr_____f

9. dec_____t

10. _____ther

11. misch_____vous

12. s_____ve

13. requ_____m

14. fr_____nd

15. n_____ce

16. for_____gn

17. f_____gn

18. conc_____ve

19. s_____ge

20. n_____ther

21. anx_____ty

22. rec_____pt

23. dec_____ve

24. h_____ght

25. s_____ze

17.4 Spelling with *ie* and *ei*

■ *Fill in the blanks in the following words with* **ie** *or* **ei**.

EXAMPLE

prem_*ie*_r

1. defic_____ncy

2. f_____ld

3. retr_____ve

4. furr_____r

5. gr_____vance

6. y_____ld

7. ach_____ve

8. d_____gn

9. fr_____ght

10. h_____r

11. pr_____st

12. y_____ld

13. n_____ghbor

14. r_____gn

15. sl_____gh

16. omnisc_____nt

17. h_____nous

18. bel_____ve

19. perc_____ve

20. bes_____ge

21. l_____sure

22. c_____ling

23. mil_____u

24. t_____r

25. G_____ger counter

17.5 Plurals

■ *Form the plural for each of the following nouns. If there is more than one plural form, give all of them. Consult your dictionary when in doubt.*

EXAMPLE

bush _____ *bushes* _____

1. reply _____

2. money _____

3. trepidation _____

4. bastion _____

5. bureaucracy _____

6. cargo _____

7. corona _____

8. thief _____

9. antenna _____

10. oasis _____

11. antithesis _____

12. half _____

13. hero _____

14. committee _____

15. beau _____

16. aquarium _____

17. essay _____

18. cemetery _____

19. embargo _____

20. locust _____

21. volley _____

22. alumnus _____

23. index _____

24. medium _____

25. criterion _____

Hyphenation and Syllabication

Use a hyphen in certain compound words and in words divided at the end of a line.

It is best to consult a dictionary to determine whether a compound word is hyphenated or is written as one or two words. Hyphenate a compound of two or more words used as a single modifier before a noun.

HYPHEN

He is a *well-known* millionaire.

NO HYPHEN

The millionaire is *well known*.

Hyphenate spelled-out compound numbers from *twenty-one* through *ninety-nine*.

When hyphenating a word at the end of a line, do not divide one-syllable words, do not put a one-letter syllable on a separate line (*a-long*, for example), and avoid carrying over a two-letter suffix to another line (*arriv-ed*). Divide words according to the syllabication in the dictionary.

18.1 Hyphenation and Syllabication

■ *Write the correct spelling of the following compounds in the blanks at the right. If a spelling is correct, write **C** in the blank. Consult a dictionary.*

EXAMPLES

hat-less _____ *hatless* _____

reenter _____ *re-enter* _____

1. road-side _____

2. now-a-days _____

3. software _____

4. eighty five _____

5. queen size _____

6. de escalate _____

7. one-hundred _____

8. hot air balloon _____

9. nation wide _____

10. laissez faire _____

11. baby sitter _____

12. one-twelfth _____

13. half truth _____

14. re print _____

15. per cent _____

16. non fiction _____

17. a six question form _____

18. ice cream cone _____

19. long-distance telephone call _____

20. great grandmother _____

21. pro American _____

22. all-purpose _____

23. re-write _____

24. excouncilman _____

25. stock-broker _____

18.2 Hyphenation and Syllabication

■ *Circle errors in hyphenation or syllabication and correct them. Add hyphens where necessary.*

EXAMPLE
The once-popular convertible is again on the market.

1. The cashier short-changed the customer.

2. The Spanish speaking nations of North America include many different ethnic groups.

3. A trouble shooter came from the maintenance department.

4. We had a long and involved discussion in class today over the u-sage of a word in our textbook.

5. When I met Susan, I knew she was a-born leader.

6. Physicians warn that quack remedies for arthritis—apple-cider, vinegar, a dry-climate, or a copper-bracelet—have no medical value.

7. Bills de-signed to ex-pand the active work force have been introduced in the House-of-Representatives.

8. Some political theorists believe that the attorney-general should be independent of the White-House, and a congressional subcommittee is studying this suggestion.

9. The Department of Public Safety tries to discourage hitch hikers because many of them are victimized by so called Good Samaritan drivers.

10. An increase of white collar jobs, a decrease of blue collar jobs, and an increase in the number of working wives will mean that 30 percent of all American families will earn $25,000 or more by 1990.

Apostrophes, Capital Letters,
Abbreviations, and Numbers

APOSTROPHES

Use the apostrophe for the possessive case of many nouns, for contractions, omissions, and for some plurals.

Use 's for the possessive of nouns not ending in s.

SINGULAR   PLURAL
   book's, Albert's   people's, children's

Use 's or ' without the s for possessive of singular nouns ending in s. Do not add the s when a singular noun ending in s is followed by a word that begins with s.

   Dennis's, or Dennis' *but not* Dennis's stories

Use ' without the s to form the possessive of plural nouns ending in s.

   the Wilsons' mailbox, the players' strategies

Use 's to form the possessive of indefinite pronouns.

   anyone's, everybody's, neither's

Use 's with only the last noun when indicating joint possession in a pair or series.

   Michael and Sherri's wedding was beautiful. (They share the wedding.)
   Michael's and Sherri's parents attended. (They do not share parents.)

Use ' to show omissions or to form contractions.

   the '80s, won't, it's (it is)

Use 's to form the plural of numerals, letters, and words being named.

   five 9's, three *b*'s

CAPITAL LETTERS

Use a capital letter to begin a sentence and to designate a proper noun.

Capitalize the first word in a sentence, the letter *I,* and the interjection *O.*

What, O what, have I done?

Capitalize the first, last, and important words in titles, including the second part of hyphenated words.

> *Great Expectations*
> *The Man with the Golden Horn*
> *Slaughterhouse-Five*

Capitalize first words in quotations and words capitalized by the author.

> "We could call this the Age of Indifference," the author wrote.

Capitalize titles preceding names.

> Lord Mountbatten

Capitalize titles of the leader of a nation even when the name of the person is not given. Capitalize titles that substitute for specific names.

> The Prime Minister is in conference.
> General Ames has been in Europe. The General has been inspecting NATO units.

A title not followed by a name is usually not capitalized.

> The secretary read the minutes of the last meeting.

Titles that are common nouns naming an office are not capitalized.

> A private has a hard life.

Capitalize degrees and titles after names.

> Bill Davis, Director of Admissions
> Martha Blount, C.P.A.

Capitalize words of family relationships used as names when not preceded by a possessive pronoun.

> Have you seen Mom?

Capitalize proper nouns and their derivatives.

> Paris, Parisian; the Southwest; Democrats, the Democratic Party; the Missouri River; Middle Atlantic States

Capitalize movements, periods, and events in history.

the Romantic Movement, the Civil War

Capitalize words referring to the Deity, to religious denominations, and to religious literature. Pronouns referring to the Deity are usually capitalized.

> God, Methodism, the Bible
> We know He is our God.

Capitalize the titles of specific courses and the names of languages.

> Biology 126, Music 240
> Mathematics 101 *but* a mathematics course (because not specific)

ABBREVIATIONS

Avoid most abbreviations in writing. Spell out the names of days, months, units of measurement, and (except in addresses) states and countries. In addresses use the abbreviations of the U.S. Postal Service (NY, CA, TX).

> Monday (*not* Mon.); February (*not* Feb.); ounce (*not* oz.); Fort Worth, Texas (*not* TX)

Abbreviations are acceptable before names (Mr., Dr.), after names (Sr., D.D.S.), and with dates and time (B.C., A.D. and A.M., P.M.).

NUMBERS

Spell out numbers that can be written in one word or two words.

> thirty-two
> two million

Use figures for other numbers.

> 12,367, $978.34, 3⅓

Never begin sentences with figures. Rephrase the sentence or spell the numbers out.

NOT
> 50 men started work.

BUT
> Fifty men started work.

OR
> There were fifty men who started work.

Use numerals for figures in a series.

We bought 10 pounds of potatoes, 2 quarts of milk, and 2 dozen eggs.

Use figures for dates, street numbers, page references, percentages, and hours of the day used with A.M. or P.M.

USE FIGURES	SPELL OUT
March 7, 1981	the seventh of March
4511 Mary Ellen Avenue	Tenth Street
See page 10.	The book has twenty pages
He paid 10 percent interest	
The meeting starts at 10 P.M.	The meeting starts at ten o'clock

19.1 The Apostrophe

■ *Give the singular possessive and the plural possessive of the following nouns.*

EXAMPLE
campaign   *campaign's*   *campaigns'*

	SINGULAR POSSESSIVE	PLURAL POSSESSIVE
1. child	_____	_____
2. wife	_____	_____
3. state	_____	_____
4. Rivera (last name)	_____	_____
5. university	_____	_____
6. Kent (last name)	_____	_____
7. genius	_____	_____
8. Perez (last name)	_____	_____
9. druggist	_____	_____
10. spectator	_____	_____
11. heroine	_____	_____
12. cemetery	_____	_____
13. chairman of the board	_____	_____
14. girl	_____	_____
15. fox	_____	_____
16. church	_____	_____
17. Mathis (last name)	_____	_____
18. attorney	_____	_____

19. mother-in-law _____ _____

20. workman _____ _____

21. baby _____ _____

22. Pakistani _____ _____

23. leaf _____ _____

24. library _____ _____

25. scientist _____ _____

19.2 The Apostrophe

■ *Add apostrophes where necessary and circle incorrect apostrophes. Change spellings where appropriate.*

EXAMPLES

Most peoples⊘opinions are based on feelings, not facts. (apostrophe precedes the *s* because *people* is plural)

Roger often complained about the demand⊘s of his busy schedule. (*demand* is not possessive)

1. Hundreds of toy's built on our main plants assembly line were returned because they were defective.

2. Many residents' of Miami, Florida, still remember the hurricane of 26, which destroyed or damaged hundreds of homes' in the area.

3. Both player's strategies were well conceived, but their techniques' needed polish.

4. Charles attitude toward his fellow workers changed when he knew them better and began to spend his evening's with them.

5. Julio and Marias' new home is beautifully landscaped with azaleas, holly, and juniper.

6. Most of an attorneys day—from eight oclock until two oclock—is spent in hearings, committee meetings, and court sessions.

7. The groom followed his future father-in-laws advice and carefully hid his car before the wedding days festivities.

8. The calculator sputtered and erroneously registered eight 7s across the screen, and these were immediately followed by a series of *E*s.

9. The children said the toys were their's, not the neighbors children's.

10. The quarterbacks and the wide receivers intuitions about their opponents plays made them an extraordinarily effective offensive combination.

19.3 Capitals

■ *Correct the errors in capitalization.*

EXAMPLE
Video *C*assette *R*ecorders and *H*ome *C*omputers are becoming less expensive.

1. The empire state building in New York City was once the world's tallest skyscraper.

2. Harvard college was founded on october 28, 1637.

3. Many impressive examples of gothic architecture dot the french countryside.

4. Many critics believe that Educational Television has matured because of its excellent production of Children's Programs.

5. The climax of Shakespeare's *King Richard III* comes when king Richard says, "a horse! a horse! my kingdom for a horse!"

6. The great lakes are connected with the atlantic ocean by the st. lawrence river and with the gulf of mexico by the illinois waterway.

7. Summer Stock Companies often make up in *esprit de corps* what they lack in theatrical sophistication and experience.

8. Winston Churchill, prime minister of great Britain during the second world war, was the author of a book on Art called *Painting for Pleasure*.

9. Eric Arthur Blair, known to the Public as George Orwell, was a British Essayist who satirized modern politicians for their use of such phrases as *render inoperative, militate against, make contact with, be subjected to,* and *make itself felt.*

10. The septuagint, one of the earliest texts of the bible, is the oldest Greek version of the old testament; Legend says that it was translated by seventy jewish scholars under the sponsorship of Ptolemy II of Egypt.

19.4 Abbreviations and Numbers

■ *Correct unacceptable usage of abbreviations and numbers. Write corrections above the line.*

EXAMPLE
We caught ~~40~~ *forty* fish ~~&~~ *and* sailed for home.

1. Few Americans know how many qts. are in a liter.

2. 35% of our stock was sold the 1st day the store opened.

3. When we retire in 96, we plan to move to a small town just outside Denver, Colo.

4. The Metro. Transit Authority purchased 22 new buses for two million, four hundred, forty thousand dollars.

5. Occupancy rates of hotels in some resort areas climbed as high as 90% during the Bicentennial celebration.

6. One lineman weighed two hundred fifty lbs.; another, two hundred forty lbs.; the third, two hundred sixty lbs.; and the last, two hundred eighty lbs.—all for an average weight of 257 pt. 5 lbs.

7. Robert flew from Jacksonville, Fla., to Atlanta, then caught a flight to L.A. after a 4-hour delay.

8. Economists agree that countries with fifty percent inflation are in deep financial trouble.

9. After reading the first 100 pp. of *War and Peace*, I had to write down the characters' names to keep from confusing them.

10. Rev. Smith, Sen. Martinez, and Capt. Briggs of the A.F. were present for the commissioning of the new Lts.

19.5 Numbers and Capitals: Review

■ *Correct all errors in capitalization, abbreviations, and the use of numbers in the following paragraph.*

The swamps and bayous of the La. coast are home to the Cajuns. These french-speaking descendants of nova scotians came to this region near the gulf of Mexico over two hundred and twenty years ago. Many of their traditional foods—Shrimp creole, Gumbo, and Jambalaya—have long been popular. Their traditional music, once ignored and in danger of dying out, has recently enjoyed a surge of popularity. Called *zydeco*, it has influenced both Country and Rock music alike.

DICTION AND STYLE

THE DICTIONARY

Dictionaries contain information that is necessary for precise writing. The following entry from the *American Heritage Dictionary* for the word *bureaucrat* indicates the kinds of information that are found in an entry. The numbers in brackets have been added.

> **bu·reau·crat** [1] (byŏor'ə-krăt') [2] *n.* [3] 1. An official of a bureaucracy. 2. Any official who insists on rigid adherence to rules, forms, and routines. [4]—**bu'reau·crat'ic** *adj.* —**bu'reau·crat'i·cal·ly** *adv.*
>
> [5] *Usage:* In American usage *bureaucrat* is almost invariably derogatory, unless the context establishes otherwise.

After the word is the following information: (1) the pronunciation and syllabication of the word, (2) the part of speech, (3) the definitions of the word, (4) the ways the word is spelled for other parts of speech, and (5) the way the word is used.

Dictionaries also include the following:

1. Principal parts of regular and irregular verbs, degrees of adjectives and adverbs, and irregular forms of nouns
2. Comparative and superlative degrees of adjectives and adverbs
3. Plurals of nouns
4. Archaic forms of inflected verbs (*doest* for the second-person present tense of *do*)
5. Labels for the technical or limited use of words (*chemistry* or *sports*, for example)
6. Other labels indicating restricted usage (*nonstandard, slang, poetic, foreign languages*)
7. Cross-references to other words and spelling variations
8. Etymologies
9. Synonyms
10. Standard abbreviations
11. Miscellaneous information, including references to famous people, to geographic areas, and to important historical movements and periods.

USAGE

Standard English is the accepted language of English-speaking people. In formal writing, avoid using informal words. Replace nonstandard words in most kinds of prose. Read the labels in a current dictionary.

NOT

She was fired up about her new job.

BUT

She was excited about her new job.

IMPROPRIETIES

Improprieties are the uses of words as the wrong parts of speech or the incorrect uses of words for similar words that have different meanings.

IMPROPRIETY	PROPER FORMS
ice tea (noun for adjective)	iced tea
easy understood (adjective for adverb)	easily understood
a quite morning	a quiet morning
new personal	new personnel

IDIOMS

Idioms are accepted expressions with meanings that differ from the meanings of the individual words themselves.

The actor told his co-star to go on stage and *break a leg*. (do her best)

Many idioms are incorrect because the wrong prepositions are used.

INCORRECT	CORRECT
conform with	conform to
oblivious to	oblivious of
in reference with	in reference to
the year of 1981	the year 1981

TRITENESS

Triteness includes worn-out or hackneyed phrases and figures of speech. Substitutes that are fresh and original should be used. Avoid such expressions as the following.

tried and true	out in left field
rhyme or reason	last but not least
slowly but surely	one in a million

EXACTNESS

Correct usage requires a knowledge of idioms, the use of a current dictionary, and wide experience with words. Words must be used precisely; writers should avoid using words that are confusing or vague.

Many people today diet in an effort to become *lanky*. (A better choice would be *slender*.)

He was in difficult *straights*. (The word should be *straits*, meaning a difficult situation.)

20.1 The Dictionary and Usage

■ *Look up each word in parentheses in a current dictionary to determine the correct choice. Underline the answer and write a summary of the statement about usage given in the dictionary.*

EXAMPLE

The television (<u>medium</u>, media) has benefited greatly from satellite broad-casting.

medium; refers to one kind of communication method
media; plural form for more than one kind

1. One of the worst effects of the earthquake, (beside, besides) the general destruction, was the devastating fire.

   _____

   _____

   _____

2. (Since, Being as) the reading assignment is rather lengthy, we will need to get an early start.

   _____

   _____

3. Although the flags of the United States and North Korea are quite (different than, different from) each other, they use the same three colors.

   _____

   _____

   _____

4. After eating *sushi*, a Japanese specialty consisting of raw fish, the tourist complained that she did not feel (good, well).

   _____

   _____

5. According to the booklet a carefully written résumé, neat clothing, and a pleasant manner are the (criterion, criteria) for a successful job interview.

_____

_____

_____

6. Shakespeare asks in one of his sonnets whether he should compare his love (to, with) a summer's day.

_____

_____

_____

7. (Regardless, Irregardless) of his questionable political beliefs, Ezra Pound remains an important twentieth-century poet.

_____

_____

_____

8. Possessing only one horn, the fabled unicorn was a (unique, most unique) creature.

_____

_____

_____

9. The debater who (inferred, implied) that his opponent was poorly prepared was disqualified for making personal remarks.

_____

_____

_____

10. The kangaroo is one (kind of, kind of a) marsupial found only in Australia.

_____

_____

20.2 The Dictionary and Usage

■ *Look up each word in parentheses in a current dictionary to determine the correct choice. Underline the answer and write a summary of the usage rule under each sentence.*

1. (Fewer, Less) than half of the presidents of the United States were born outside the original thirteen colonies.

   _____

   _____

   _____

2. Unshaven and red-eyed, the newspaper editor looked (as if, like) he had worked for days without sleep.

   _____

   _____

   _____

3. The flowerpot fell (off, off of) the ledge and smashed on the sidewalk.

   _____

   _____

   _____

4. At the turn of the century only a small (percent, percentage) of people owned automobiles.

   _____

   _____

   _____

5. When we came (inside, inside of) the arena, we were deafened by the roar of the crowd.

   _____

_____

_____

6. The accident victim was only (partly, partially) covered by insurance.

_____

_____

_____

7. For the coffee merchant, inhaling the aroma of the Colombian beans was a (sensuous, sensual) pleasure.

_____

_____

_____

8. The cache of arrowheads indicated that (sometime, some time) in the past a tribe of primitive Indians had encamped on the banks of the river.

_____

_____

_____

9. The customer complained that (these kinds, these kind) of socks stretch out of shape after the first washing.

_____

_____

_____

10. Many gardeners use different types of mulches to (try and, try to) keep their gardens weed-free.

_____

_____

_____

20.3 The Dictionary and Usage

■ *Look up each word in parentheses in a current dictionary to determine the correct choice. Underline the answer and write a summary of the usage rule under each sentence.*

1. Thousands of tourists visit Niagara Falls (everyday, every day) during the summer months.

   _____

   _____

   _____

2. Parents quickly learn to deal with skinned knees, runny noses, and other (everyday, every day) problems without becoming needlessly upset.

   _____

   _____

   _____

3. The rock star had so great an (affect, effect) on his audience that three people fainted.

   _____

   _____

   _____

4. The contractor (agreed to, agreed with) the replacement of the kitchen floor.

   _____

   _____

   _____

5. I was surprised to learn that the temperature of an oven drops about twenty-five degrees (every, ever) time the door is opened.

   _____

6. The hot, thirsty campers saw the glimmer of a waterfall a long (way, ways) off.

_____

_____

_____

7. Although she was trained in cellular biology, the graduate student found it difficult to distinguish (among, between) three species of bacteria.

_____

_____

_____

8. After studying for (awhile, a while), the students ordered a pizza.

_____

_____

_____

9. The author felt so (bad, badly) after the disappointing reviews of his book that he vowed never to write again.

_____

_____

_____

10. The audience laughed as the clown (busted, burst, bursted) the balloon.

_____

_____

_____

20.4 The Dictionary and Usage

■ *Look up each word in parentheses in a current dictionary to determine the correct choice. Underline the answer and write a summary of the usage rule under each sentence.*

1. After a local referendum the dome of the (capital, capitol) building was cleaned and repaired.

   _____

   _____

   _____

2. The cheerleaders were so (enthused, enthusiastic) about the touchdown that they performed double somersaults.

   _____

   _____

   _____

3. After being rescued from the burning house, the family pets were frightened, but (alright, all right).

   _____

   _____

   _____

4. Because of a shortage of bamboo shoots, (fewer, less) pandas than expected will survive a severe winter.

   _____

   _____

   _____

5. The ballet had (already, all ready) begun by the time we arrived.

   _____

_____

_____

6. The interior designer (complemented, complimented) the blue sofa with a green and turquoise rug.

_____

_____

_____

7. Peter Minuit bought Manhattan (off, off of, from) the Man-a-hat-a Indians for trinkets worth about twenty-four dollars.

_____

_____

_____

8. City dwellers grow used to the (continual, continuous) sound of backfiring cars and honking horns.

_____

_____

_____

9. The reason James Bond movies are so popular is (because, that) they combine the appeal of traditional spy stories with the appeal of technological gadgetry.

_____

_____

_____

10. The producer said that (irregardless, regardless) of the worth of the play, ticket sales would determine the length of its run.

_____

_____

_____

20.5 The Dictionary and Usage

■ *Underline each example of poor usage and write the correction underneath each sentence.*
No sentence contains more than two such examples. One sentence is correct.

EXAMPLE
The executive complained that the attempt to *finalize those sort* of deals was frustrating.

formalize; those sorts

1. Compared to an Afghan hound, whose long, fine fur needs careful grooming every day, a German shepherd is easy to care for.

2. Over two million boys in America are effected by hyperactivity, a disorder that some believe contributes later to alcoholism.

3. The grateful owner divided the reward between the three girls who found and returned his lost pet.

4. The reason the barbershop quartet performed so many nostalgic numbers is because the audience requested those sort.

5. Going to the circus to see the clown Emmett Kelley perform his unique act—a bumbling attempt to sweep a spotlight into a sack— is the kind of a memory to be cherished by the theatergoer.

6. The Ferris wheel whirled all together too fast like it was about to spin away into the sky.

7. Most of the refugees who emigrate to the United States eventually find productive and satisfying jobs.

8. Fewer than half of the people who attended the opening night of *Aida* wore formal dress; consequently, sequined dresses appeared besides corduroy jeans.

_____

9. The newspaper reader inferred from the interview that since everyone who ate the chicken salad felt badly, all were suffering from food poisoning.

_____

10. The student who completed less than half of the problem was given credit for what she had done correctly.

_____

20.6 The Dictionary and Usage

■ *Underline each example of poor usage and write the correction underneath each sentence. No sentence contains more than two such examples.*

1. Many people suffered so badly from smallpox during the eighteenth century that contemporary writers compared the disease with a tidal wave destroying everything in its path.

   _____

2. The theater manager asked the audience to be patient for a while until the leading man, who had fallen off of a ladder, could be replaced by an understudy.

   _____

3. The reviewer implied that audiences at the turn of the century were naive because they enjoyed the kind of a play known as melodrama.

   _____

4. The criteria used by the testing agency to establish new tire safety involves determining the amount of air pressure that will bust a tire.

   _____

5. A brownout is when lights are partially dimmed or extinguished because of a power reduction.

   _____

6. One criteria of a good newspaper is balanced yet aggressive reporting.

   _____

7. Because of the unnaturally warm weather, a large amount of camellias were already to bloom before the frost.

   _____

8. The reason the water pump will not work is because it has not been used for some time.

_____

9. Hanging from the ceiling at the party was a *piñata*, a colorful paper ball that, when bursted, showered candies and small toys between the laughing children.

_____

10. The yellow jacket is one type wasp that sometimes build its nests underground.

_____

20.7 The Dictionary and Usage

■ *Underline each example of poor usage and write the corrections above each line.*

One of the most exciting events of the nineteenth century was a rather unique industrial world's fair held in the Crystal Palace in London, a glass building that looked all together fragile but was, in fact, very strong. A large percent of the populace were so enthused about the display that some attended the show several times. Inside the transparent building they were treated to extensive displays of machinery and furniture; textiles were hanged from the ceiling, and exotic plants were clustered in small groups all the ways down the central aisle. It was difficult for the viewer to try and choose between the hundreds of exhibits, all so plentiful and so highly decorated that they had a dazzling affect on the eyes.

20.8 The Dictionary and Usage

■ *Underline each example of poor usage and write the corrections above each line.*

A large amount of people would agree to the idea that going to the
circus was an exciting childhood event. The atmosphere itself had a
special tang; even the sawdust hanging in the air was a sensual pleasure
as if, for awhile, one could both smell and taste the excitement. What
a thrill it was when the lights dimmed and the trapeze artist flew over
the crowds like a bird on the wing, and how the audience jumped when
the clown suddenly bursted a balloon filled with water! Surely nothing
can compare to the heart-stopping experience of seeing the unprotected
lion tamer taunting the king of the beasts, who, snarling and growling,
was ready to hurl himself off of the ledge in his cage. Irregardless of
the time, the end always came too quickly; parents were already to
leave while children still sat starry-eyed, clutching the remains of sticky
candied apples or crumpled bags of popcorn.

20.9 The Dictionary and Standard English

■ *With the aid of a dictionary, label the italicized words as* **formal, informal, colloquial,** *and so on. Replace substandard expressions with equivalents in Standard English.*

EXAMPLE

The mechanic said he was *fixing to* begin work on my car. _regional; about_

1. Many prospectors passed *thru* British Columbia on their way to the Yukon during the famous Klondike gold rush. _____

2. The Lincoln Memorial is *mighty* impressive any time but especially at night when the crowds have departed. _____

3. One can earn *plenty* of extra income by selling scrap aluminum. _____

4. Occasionally some misguided *punks* vandalize public property. _____

5. The irate coach, *annoyed* by questionable decisions of the officials, decided to protest. _____

6. Gentrification of the inner cities has indirectly made life harder for people on *skid row* by eliminating many of the flophouses where they live. _____

7. The old woman remained *chipper* despite her hardships and declining health. _____

8. I was certainly *put out* by her rude behavior. _____

9. I do not want to *wrangle* with you over this matter, but I think you are wrong. _____

10. Something *fishy* is going on here, and I feel uncomfortable. _____

20.10 The Dictionary and Standard English

■ *For each of the following supply an appropriate expression in Standard English.*

EXAMPLE

flaky _____ *not dependable* _____

1. double-cross _____

2. whodunit _____

3. lousy _____

4. plain as day _____

5. goldbrick _____

6. lots of _____

7. elbow grease _____

8. guy _____

9. enthused _____

10. goes to show _____

11. hock _____

12. near enough of _____

13. can't hardly _____

14. would not of _____

15. couple of _____

16. set around _____

17. could of _____

18. irregardless _____

19. being as _____

20. suspicioned _____

20.11 Improprieties

■ *Circle improprieties in the following phrases and correct them in the blanks at the right. If you find none, write **C** in the blank.*

EXAMPLE

occupation hazards _____ *occupational* _____

1. reforming institution policies _____

2. especial nice _____

3. a careful developed plan _____

4. education experience _____

5. trivia incident _____

6. a poor paid employee _____

7. a wood baseball bat _____

8. a frequent used excuse _____

9. a utopia hideaway _____

10. a thin-skin person _____

11. the unstabled chemical compounds _____

12. a quiet convincing argument _____

13. the vandals who rapined Rome _____

14. an erupting volcano crevassing the hills _____

15. a resonance voice _____

16. abstracted beyond understanding _____

17. classified as an absorbent _____

18. a handwriting letter _____

19. banjoed their way to the top ten _____

20. a meander stream _____

21. dry, sand soil _____

22. holidayed the time away _____

23. the redirective coming from the officer _____

24. mystery phenomena _____

25. ivy tendoned to the walls _____

20.12 Improprieties

■ *Choose the correct word and write it in the blank at the right. Consult a dictionary if necessary.*

EXAMPLE

Only (two, to, too) species of the cat family are presently facing possible extinction in India—the Asian lion and the Bengal tiger.

two

1. She tried to (immolate, emulate) her friend's success at the office. _____

2. John had a (bailful, baleful) look after the test. _____

3. All her efforts to diet were (waisted, wasted). _____

4. My doctor gave me an (emolument, emollient) for my burned hand. _____

5. Money was available to (aid, aide) the victims of the flood. _____

6. All of the participants in the marriage workshop reported an improvement in their (marital, martial) relationships. _____

7. Many people buy (navel, naval) oranges because they are usually seedless. _____

8. The (principle, principal) reason for Margaret's resignation was her strong objection to the new budget. _____

9. She made an (object, abject) apology for her behavior. _____

10. Most geologists divide the latest era of geologic time into seven (epics, epochs). _____

11. Fried fish and (cole, coal, cold) slaw are a favorite culinary combination. _____

12. The sun can burn human skin even on cloudy days; (its, it's) ultraviolet rays easily penetrate cloud cover. _____

13. The dieter tried to reduce his (wasteline, waist-line). _____

14. The coaching staff of some football teams hire professional psychologists to help motivate (their, there) players. _____

15. Setting a new record at the marathon was a great (fete, feat) for the runner. _____

16. Only a few students caught the professor's pass-ing (allusion, illusion) to Norse mythology. _____

17. (Passed, Past) over by all the political pundits, the darkhorse candidate emerged the winner of the state primary. _____

18. (Preceding, Proceeding) along migratory routes, wild geese often fly in easily recognizable for-mations. _____

19. Physicians (prescribe, proscribe) antibiotics for most respiratory infections. _____

20. His cowardly actions during the latest crisis can-not be described as anything other than (con-temptuous, contemptible). _____

21. The anthropologist had spent five years studying the fertility (rights, rites) of three small tribes liv-ing in the Amazon basin. _____

22. The general (moral, morale) of the nation usually increases after a presidential election. _____

23. The delighted parents welcomed their son's (fi-ancé, fiancée) with warmth and affection. _____

24. The city was (greatful, grateful) for the contribu-tions to the library fund. _____

25. The law rarely accepts the argument that the in-dividual's (conscience, conscious) should be the guide to acceptable social behavior. _____

20.13 Improprieties

■ *Choose the correct word and write it in the blank at the right. Consult a dictionary if necessary.*

EXAMPLE
I want to know where (there, their) comments will appear. *their*

1. After her coronation, she (reined, reigned) for the remainder of the year. _____

2. The speaker made a (moot, mute) point in his lecture. _____

3. Although the leopard stalks its (prey, pray) carefully, it is unsuccessful more often than not. _____

4. The prosecutor described the (scene, seen) so powerfully that everyone in the courtroom was moved. _____

5. A good salad often has (leeks, leaks) in it. _____

6. The policeman (sighted, cited, sited) the suspicious-looking man for loitering. _____

7. As soon as the marooned sailors (sighted, cited, sited) the search plane, they began waving frantically. _____

8. This is (to, too) much excitement to bear. _____

9. My bonus was larger (then, than) I had expected. _____

10. The two rams (abutted, butted) heads. _____

11. The (plane, plain) the cowboys crossed extends across most of two states. _____

12. I hate to see someone (flout, flaunt) wealth. _____

13. The new producer has recruited writers throughout the region and claims they write good (material, materiel). _____

14. The (merry, marry) wedding guests showered the bride and groom with rice.

_____

15. Her story does not (gibe, jibe) with the truth.

_____

16. Many people object to (corporal, corporeal) punishment.

_____

17. The legislators met at the (capital, capitol) rotunda.

_____

18. Jeff's many (condensations, condescensions) alienated him from friends.

_____

19. The American language obtains many (lonewords, loanwords) from other languages.

_____

20. The passenger paid her (fare, fair) and walked to a seat on the bus.

_____

21. The Soviet Union is (comprised, composed) of fifteen different republics.

_____

22. When the golfer hit the ball into the woods, he cried out, "(Four, Fore)!"

_____

23. Philip asked the antique dealer if he would (sell, sale) the oak wardrobe.

_____

24. The Academic (Council, Counsel) discussed the new curriculum.

_____

25. When the driver's car stalled, she quickly placed (flairs, flares) on the highway.

_____

20.14 Idioms

■ *Circle faulty idioms in the following sentences. Write correct idioms in the blanks at the right.*

EXAMPLE
Your house looks very similar (with) ours.   *to*

1. In the year of 1922 T. S. Eliot published one of the most influential poems of the century.   _____

2. The food value of pork is comparable toward the food value of chicken.   _____

3. Oblivious to possible dangers, the unpredictable grizzly bear will charge even a man.   _____

4. Many teachers find that attractive classrooms are conducive of learning.   _____

5. The puma and the wolf were once indigenous of almost every state in the union.   _____

6. The coming election has a bearing with almost all congressional action.   _____

7. Americans' replies to the challenges of periods of crisis usually are of the affirmative.   _____

8. The three panelists maintained a lively dialogue to the audience.   _____

9. I read the book from cover to conclusion.   _____

10. Surprised with the suggestion, I could only promise to study it carefully later.   _____

20.15 Idioms

■ *Circle faulty idioms in the following sentences. Write correct idioms in the blanks at the right. Write **C** if the idiom is correct.*

EXAMPLE

How long have you been waiting (on) your friends?   *for*

1. Bobby has an irritating habit of borrowing money off his friends.   _____

2. We jointed the two pieces of steel.   _____

3. The parents doted in their children.   _____

4. We decided to turn away the offer on our home.   _____

5. The members of the research team went past the call of duty as they tried to complete the project before the upcoming deadline.   _____

6. When it comes to playing tennis, I am superior over everyone in my class.   _____

7. The trip was not all that interesting.   _____

8. The reason the dam broke is because of the heavy spring rains.   _____

9. In regards to the city's problems, the mayor will call a council meeting.   _____

10. I had been visiting to a friend's house when the alarm sounded.   _____

20.16 Triteness

■ *Revise the following sentences to eliminate triteness.*

EXAMPLE

I decided to take the bull by the horns.

I decided to confront the problem.

1. The Bullets were walking on air after they won the Little League championship.

2. She was a fair-weather friend who was never around in the clinches.

3. Enlistment in the military grew by leaps and bounds during the first few weeks of World War II.

4. "You have bought during a declining market," said the doleful stockbroker to her disheartened client, "but if at first you don't succeed, try, try again."

5. San Francisco, a city that was rebuilt after suffering the effects of a devastating earthquake, is proof that every cloud has a silver lining.

6. Old diaries, journals, and letters reveal that the early pioneers in the West found some of the wild country to be pretty as a picture.

_____

_____

_____

7. The chief targets of confidence men are gullible investors who continue to believe that there is a pot of gold at the end of the rainbow.

_____

_____

_____

8. While traveling down the highway of life, one must remember that virtue is its own reward.

_____

_____

_____

9. The thrust of most economists' complaints is that short-range political considerations take precedence over long-range economic policy.

_____

_____

_____

10. Good accounts are worth their weight in gold in the current business climate.

_____

_____

_____

20.17 Triteness

■ *Revise the following sentences to eliminate triteness.*

EXAMPLE

Jerome's explanation got him out of the frying pan and into the fire.

Jerome's explanation got him into even more serious trouble.

1. This author's discussion of the causes of the Russo-Japanese War really hit the nail on the head.

   _____

   _____

2. The United States traditionally has been in the forefront of medical research.

   _____

   _____

   _____

3. Superstars of the college sports scene, in a manner of speaking, can write their own tickets in professional sports.

   _____

   _____

   _____

4. The first British colonists in America quickly learned that charity and neighborliness were necessary to keep the ball rolling.

   _____

   _____

   _____

5. A few of these first colonists gave up the ship and returned to England, but most never lost heart.

   _____

6. Those willing to travel in the wee hours of the morning usually spend less for airline fares.

_____

_____

_____

7. The doctor assured me after my last checkup that I was as sound as a dollar.

_____

_____

_____

8. The main duty of the public health officer is to nip communicable diseases in the bud.

_____

_____

_____

9. Some people deliberately muddy the water every time they speak.

_____

_____

_____

10. The batter slammed the ball into the outfield, raced to first, and then cut for second, running at lightning speed.

_____

_____

_____

Wordiness and Repetition

WORDINESS

Avoid using many words when one or two will serve.

> The envelope containing the electric bill was delivered today. (nine words)
> The electric bill came today. (five words)

Avoid overuse of the passive voice.

> A red car was seen by witnesses. (seven words)
> Witnesses saw a red car. (five words)

Revise long sentences to achieve concision.

> I wish to say that I have not at this moment fully engaged in this warlike action. (seventeen words)
> I have not yet begun to fight. (seven words)

Avoid dependence on *it is, there is,* and *there are.*

> It is essential for the house to be painted.
> The house must be painted.
> There are only two application forms left.
> Only two application forms are left.

REPETITION

Avoid excessive repetition of words, synonyms, and sounds.

> The book on the table is a book about buccaneers in the South Seas.
> The book on the table is about buccaneers in the South Seas.
> The wind sifted sparks from the sizzling blaze.
> The wind blew sparks from the blaze.

21.1 Wordiness

■ *Revise the following sentences to make them concise.*

EXAMPLE

Alison spoke in a forceful manner.

Alison spoke forcefully.

1. It was William Harvey who first wrote about the circulation of the blood.

2. In terms of the size of its land, Canada is the second largest country in the world.

3. To be sure, Benjamin Franklin was not, as it were, a great writer, but he was, to all intents and purposes, a great man, more or less.

4. Americans have always applauded the tenacious underdog who is down but who tries to recover and help himself.

5. Simon Bolivar is considered by many people to be a hero because of his work in helping defeat, through armed conflict, the Spanish armies in South America.

_____

_____

_____

6. As anybody can see, most Americans have been affected by television in such a way that their appreciation of live theater has obviously become less and less.

_____

_____

_____

7. It has been shown that the length of the common cold can be reduced by giving the person with the cold doses of zinc glutonate in the form of lozenges.

_____

_____

_____

8. In the times in which we live, people just can hardly be independent any longer. Look what is happening to them in the field of education. They cannot think for themselves. This is also true in other areas of life.

_____

_____

_____

9. Looking out the window of our car, we saw the little, tiny cafe you had told us about in the letter you sent us.

_____

_____

_____

10. After reviewing the evidence in your case that was presented by your lawyer to me, we realize that there is some justification and warrant for a new trial.

_____

_____

_____

21.2 Wordiness

■ *Revise the following sentences to make them concise.*

EXAMPLE

I came for the reason that I was hungry.

I came because I was hungry.

1. In this day and age in the world in which we live, we face enormously large economic problems.

_____

_____

2. The witness's account is not considered to be trustworthy by many people.

_____

_____

3. The British leader by the name of Cornwallis was the general who was forced to surrender at Yorktown when his outnumbered troops were surrounded and could not escape by either land or sea.

_____

_____

4. Most eye-catching advertisements in magazines attract the reader's attention with designs that are bold and colors that are bright.

_____

_____

5. An ovenbird is an American bird that is a member of the warbler family and that builds a nest that resembles an oven on the floor of a forest.

_____

6. In many ways certain cities retained and still do retain a small-town atmosphere in those neighborhoods characterized by unique ethnic charm and lifestyles.

_____

_____

_____

7. For years and years the basic cultural foundation of this great nation was the small town with its small, homogeneous neighborhoods and communal cohesion.

_____

_____

_____

8. Beginning in the 1930s and continuing through several decades down to the present time, writers have often been interested in Hollywood as a setting for their novels.

_____

_____

_____

9. The water that overflowed from the plumbing in our bathroom reached the hall carpet and caused a stain on it.

_____

_____

_____

10. Two breeds of dogs that are generally considered by most authorities as good guard dogs are the Doberman pinscher and the German shepherd, and these two breeds may, without difficulty, be compared and contrasted on the grounds of appearance, disposition, and physical prowess.

21.3 Wordiness

■ *Revise the following sentences to make them concise.*

1. It is a known and proven fact that run-off elections draw fewer voters than regular elections.

   _____

   _____

   _____

2. Not many people are familiar with the little-known fact that Thomas Alva Edison was an avid reader who at the age of fifteen had read most of the books in the Detroit Public Library.

   _____

   _____

   _____

3. Let us end the festivities of the evening by all singing the song of our school.

   _____

   _____

   _____

4. Current research on the nervous system of the cockroach, of all things, might just conceivably lead to a cure for glaucoma, a disease of the eye.

   _____

   _____

   _____

5. The issue of price supports is an issue that Congress needs to settle with decisiveness.

   _____

6. Some birdfeeders differ in various ways from others because various birds have different eating habits and feeding requirements, and it is just that simple.

_____

_____

_____

7. Mammoths were prehistoric beasts that looked like elephants with very hairy skin and that often measured eleven feet at the shoulders with tusks as along as thirteen feet.

_____

_____

_____

8. Laws requiring motorcycle riders to wear crash helmets have saved, beyond any doubt or question, many lives in the past and will most certainly account for the saving of many lives in the future.

_____

_____

_____

9. I have noticed that many of the most noticeable political changes escape the notice of political commentators.

_____

_____

_____

10. The value of these new procedures will become evident to our staff within a short period of time.

_____

_____

_____

21.4 Repetition

■ *Revise the following sentences to eliminate ineffective repetition.*

EXAMPLE
All of the indicators indicate that the show will be a success.

All of the indicators suggest that the show will be a success.

1. Instant replays show that officials usually make correct calls and perform their duties both correctly and responsibly.

_____

_____

_____

2. After the bear market of the early 1970s, stockbrokers decided to diversify and to market various other securities other than common stocks.

_____

_____

_____

3. Both of the halfbacks were both agile and powerful runners.

_____

_____

_____

4. Most large cities are circumscribed by large beltways that help to decrease large traffic jams.

_____

_____

_____

5. As echoes of the shepherd's voice echoed through the valley, all nature seemed to be listening.

_____

_____

_____

6. The respected judge of a debate never allows contempt or scorn or disparagement or derision to be displayed on the debate floor.

_____

_____

_____

7. Sewing one's own clothes is a way of saving money and allows one to choose one's favorite style and one's favorite fabric.

_____

_____

_____

8. Successful football teams that win often have kickers who kick field goals and kick extra points well.

_____

_____

_____

9. House plants give a house a fresh and inviting appearance, unless too many are crowded into a small house.

_____

_____

_____

10. Farmers' markets are enjoying a good resurgence in larger cities; on good days, a farmer in New York or Seattle or Santa Fe or Boston may gross thousands of dollars.

_____

_____

_____

21.5 Repetition

■ *Revise the following sentences to eliminate ineffective repetition.*

EXAMPLE

I propose that we further study this proposal.

We need to study this proposal further.

1. The heavy debts of many debt-ridden countries are straining the debt-carrying capacity of the international monetary community.

2. Floods that flood fields and flood croplands are ever-present dangers to the farmer.

3. A cup of raisins contains almost eight times as many calories as a cup of strawberries contains.

4. Small bark beetles bear a fungus that causes a disease that attacks the Dutch elm tree.

5. Fashion designers sometimes fashion their designs after the traditional dress of nomadic tribes.

6. Horizontal stripes on clothes emphasize heaviness and are shunned by heavy people.

_____

_____

_____

7. The questions that the prosecutor asked seemed to question the witness's credibility.

_____

_____

_____

8. Sand painting, the ancient art of painting pictures with colored sand, was first originated by American Indians for their ancient rituals.

_____

_____

_____

9. Some elk from overpopulated elk herds in Yellowstone National Park have been exported to other parks in other regions and even to other countries.

_____

_____

_____

10. Charcoal, first used as a filter in gas masks during the First World War, filters the air in submarines and spacecraft and also filters automobile emissions.

_____

_____

_____

Connotation, Figurative Language, Flowery Language, and Vocabulary

CONNOTATION

Words often have special associations called **connotations. Denotations** of words are their precise meanings. Denotatively, the word *home* simply refers to a dwelling place. Connotatively, the word suggests several emotional reactions relating to family, friends, and special occasions.

Good writers attempt to find words that have the right associations —those that work most effectively.

EXAMPLE
> Fred is a *funny* person. (*Funny* is weak because it is too general.)

IMPROVED
> Fred is *witty*.
>
> Fred is a *practical joker*.
>
> Fred is a *great impersonator*.

FIGURATIVE LANGUAGE

Avoid mixed and inappropriate figures of speech. Mixed figures associate things that are not logically related.

EXAMPLE
> Next he dove into a particularly dry discussion of his past experience.

IMPROVED
> Next he entered into a particularly dry discussion of his past experience.

Use figurative comparisons to create originality.

EXAMPLE
> Language is the cornerstone of civilization. (metaphor)
>
> Opportunity is *like* a good mystery story; you never know what will happen when you turn the page. (simile)

FLOWERY LANGUAGE

Avoid ornate or pretentious language. Make your sentences clear.

PLAIN LANGUAGE	FLOWERY LANGUAGE
today	in this world in which we live and work
pen	this writing instrument
finally	having reached the termination of this discourse

22.1 Connotation

■ *Words that have approximately the same denotation frequently suggest meanings that are different. The combinations that follow bring together words with different connotations. In the spaces at the right, rate each word in terms of its favorability of connotation —1 for most favorable, 2 for less favorable, and 3 for least favorable. Be prepared to defend your decisions and to explain the different shades of connotation.*

EXAMPLE

offhand _____2_____

thoughtless _____3_____

casual _____1_____

1. prudent _____

    careful _____

    cautious _____

2. perilous _____

    dangerous _____

    scary _____

3. run away _____

    escape _____

    desert _____

4. dislike _____

    disapprove _____

    detest _____

5. extravagant _____

    prodigal _____

    abundant _____

6. devout _____

    pious _____

    saintly _____

7. absurd _____

    silly _____

    preposterous _____

8. talented _____

    capable _____

    competent _____

9. quiet _____

    restful _____

    serene _____

10. pleasure _____

    amusement _____

    titillation _____

11. wither   ————

    languish   ————

    shrivel   ————

12. simple   ————

    naive   ————

    innocent   ————

13. impulsive   ————

    spontaneous   ————

    unconstrained   ————

14. famous   ————

    notorious   ————

    well-known   ————

15. venerable   ————

    aged   ————

    elderly   ————

16. bright   ————

    brainy   ————

    intelligent   ————

17. beautiful   ————

    cute   ————

    pretty   ————

18. singer   ————

    vocalist   ————

    virtuoso   ————

19. vulture   ————

    scavenger   ————

    buzzard   ————

20. venturous   ————

    hazardous   ————

    dangerous   ————

21. lie   ————

    deception   ————

    falsehood   ————

22. visionary   ————

    dreamer   ————

    romantic   ————

23. illegal   ————

    unlawful   ————

    criminal   ————

24. ignoble   ————

    vile   ————

    disreputable   ————

25. request   ————

    solicit   ————

    beg   ————

NAME _____

DATE _____ SCORE _____

22.2 Connotation

■ *Words that have approximately the same denotation frequently suggest meanings that are different. The combinations that follow bring together words with different connotations. In the spaces at the right, rate each word in terms of its favorability of connotation —1 for most favorable, 2 for less favorable, and 3 for least favorable. Be prepared to defend your decisions and to explain the different shades of connotation.*

EXAMPLE

rehearse   _1_

practice   _2_

drill   _3_

1. force   _____
   compel   _____
   coerce   _____

2. temperate   _____
   self-denying _____
   austere   _____

3. offensive   _____
   repulsive   _____
   revolting   _____

4. haggard   _____
   cadaverous   _____
   wasted   _____

5. employee   _____
   worker   _____
   laborer   _____

6. part   _____
   separate _____
   sever   _____

7. intentions _____
   design   _____
   end   _____

8. expedition _____
   junket   _____
   trip   _____

9. motive   _____
   incentive _____
   inducement _____

10. serene   _____
    calm   _____
    passionless _____

11. awkward   _____

    bungling   _____

    incompetent   _____

12. eccentricity   _____

    foible   _____

    quirk   _____

13. puny   _____

    little   _____

    small   _____

14. plead   _____

    argue   _____

    exhort   _____

15. normal   _____

    mediocre   _____

    commonplace   _____

16. resist   _____

    defy   _____

    oppose   _____

17. distinguished   _____

    noted   _____

    renowned   _____

18. wealthy   _____

    rich   _____

    opulent   _____

19. probity   _____

    candor   _____

    frankness   _____

20. habitual   _____

    customary   _____

    conventional   _____

21. alarming   _____

    frightful   _____

    scary   _____

22. choosy   _____

    selective   _____

    finicky   _____

23. imitation   _____

    counterfeit   _____

    sham   _____

24. perseverance   _____

    obstinacy   _____

    doggedness   _____

25. merchandise   _____

    hawk   _____

    peddle   _____

22.3 Figurative Language

■ *Here is a descriptive passage from Francis Parkman's* The Oregon Trail. *Fill in the blanks using the following list of Parkman's figures of speech and images.*

bellowed and growled	accompaniment	to roll hoarsely
whirling sheets	beat down	leaped out quivering
cataracts	black heads	long rolling peal
	deep muttering	piles of cotton

It was late that morning before we were on the march; and early in the afternoon we were compelled to encamp, for a thunder-gust came up and suddenly enveloped us in [1] _____ of rain. With much ado we pitched our tents amid the tempest, and all night long the thunder [2] _____ over our heads. In the morning light peaceful showers succeeded the [3] _____ of rain that had been drenching us through the canvas of our tents. About noon, when there were some treacherous indications of fair weather, we got in motion again.

Not a breath of air stirred over the free and open prairie; the clouds were like light [4] _____; and where the blue sky was visible, it wore a hazy and languid aspect. The sun [5] _____ upon us with a sultry, penetrating heat almost insupportable, and as our party crept slowly along over the interminable levels the horses hung their heads as they waded fetlock deep through the mud, and the men slouched into the easiest position upon the saddle. At last, towards evening, the old familiar [6] _____ of thunder-clouds rose fast above the horizon, and the same [7] _____ of distant thunder that had become the ordinary [8] _____ of our after- noon's journey began [9] _____ over the prairie. Only a few minutes elapsed before the whole sky was densely shrouded, and the prairie and some clusters of woods in front assumed a purple hue beneath the inky shadows. Suddenly from the densest fold of the cloud the flash [10] _____ again and again down to the edge of the prairie; and at the same instant came the sharp burst and the [11] _____ of the thunder. A cool wind, filled with the smell of rain, just then overtook us, levelling the tall grass by the side of the path.

22.4 Flowery Language

■ *Revise the following sentences to eliminate flowery language.*

EXAMPLE
The inside of a geode glitters with the silvery radiance of sidereal splendor.

The inside of a geode sparkles with crystals.

1. We looked at the puffy cotton balls in the sky.

   _____

   _____

2. As a young boy, I frequently stood rapt beneath the spangled vault of heaven, transfixed by the nocturnal cacophony of whippoorwills.

   _____

   _____

3. Many cardiologists advise a swift retreat from the ambrosial condiments of the evening repast.

   _____

   _____

   _____

4. The stirring harmonies and rousing melodic lines of John Philip Sousa's immortal march entitled "Stars and Stripes Forever" never fail to quicken my heart with patriotic fervor.

   _____

   _____

   _____

5. Many poets have been inspired by the vision of artless, cherubic children gamboling like sylvan nymphs over the verdurous sward.

   _____

6. With the coming of golden autumn the cultivators of the earth garner the blessings of Ceres.

_____

_____

_____

7. The venerable institution of holy matrimony has become the object of much sociological research in the hallowed halls of academia.

_____

_____

_____

8. The proud old scion of pioneer stock, a true son of the prairie, fondly mused upon the halcyon days of his youth when he gently guided lowing herds of lordly bovines across undulating seas of grass.

_____

_____

_____

9. The pied clouds of pastel hues served notice that the strong winds had given way to the wings of gentle zephyrs.

_____

_____

_____

10. The lofty reaches of the craggy tops of the mountains were covered by the freezing precipitation that fell in a frenzied swirl.

_____

_____

_____

22.5 Vocabulary

■ *In the blank at the right, place the letter of the word or phrase you believe is nearest in meaning to the italicized word. You may guess; then consult a dictionary.*

EXAMPLE
sumptuous meals: (a) delicious, (b) carefully prepared, (c) lavish. *c*

1. a *defunct* issue: (a) overdrawn, (b) boring, (c) dead _____

2. an *assiduous* student: (a) diligent, (b) well-read, (c) skeptical _____

3. a *cogent* argument: (a) clear, (b) concise, (c) convincing _____

4. a *quixotic* character: (a) questioning, (b) variable, (c) visionary _____

5. a *lethargic* river: (a) sluggish, (b) polluted, (c) deep _____

6. a *deleterious* comment: (a) unnecessary, (b) injurious, (c) funny _____

7. the *nadir* of my life: (a) abomination, (b) highest point, (c) lowest point _____

8. a *gratuitous* insult: (a) unwarranted, (b) deserved, (c) vehement _____

9. their *heterodox* beliefs: (a) spiritual, (b) conservative, (c) heretical _____

10. a *verbose* lecturer: (a) dynamic, (b) wordy, (c) boring _____

11. please *elucidate*: (a) explain, (b) denounce, (c) arrange _____

12. *peremptory* treatment: (a) sensitive, (b) overbearing, (c) careful _____

13. Behold the *firmament*: (a) earth, (b) sky, (c) fortification _____

14. to *opt* for freedom: (a) decide, (b) flee, (c) sing _____

15. a *disparate* group of people: (a) essentially different, (b) dangerous, (c) capable of murder _____

16. a *proletarian*: (a) wage-earner, (b) revolutionary, (c) democrat _____

17. a *laconic* reply: (a) heated, (b) ill-advised, (c) concise _____

18. to live in *straitened* circumstances: (a) limited (b) noisy, (c) pleasant _____

19. a *splenetic* personality: (a) lively, (b) forceful, (c) irritable _____

20. a *choleric* temperament: (a) sickly, (b) irascible, (c) morose _____

22.6 Vocabulary

■ *In the blank at the right, place the letter of the word or phrase you believe is nearest in meaning to the italicized word. You may guess; then consult a dictionary.*

EXAMPLE

a *repugnant* appearance: (a) colorful, (b) tasteless, (c) repulsive

_____*c*_____

1. an *aquiline* nose: (a) hooked, (b) long, (c) snub _____

2. *desultory* talk: (a) insulting, (b) boring, (c) random _____

3. a *malignant* plan: (a) ineffective, (b) evil, (c) terminal _____

4. an *overt* act: (a) subversive, (b) hostile, (c) open to view _____

5. to live in *ignominy*: (a) disgrace, (b) squalor, (c) ignorance _____

6. a *crucial* year: (a) disturbing, (b) painful, (c) decisive _____

7. a needed *admonition*: (a) reproof, (b) falsehood, (c) compliment _____

8. a *facetious* remark: (a) obvious, (b) witty, (c) angry _____

9. a *virulent* speech: (a) energetic, (b) libelous, (c) hostile _____

10. the *acrimonious* controversy: (a) bitter, (b) marital, (c) religious _____

11. an *ineradicable* mark: (a) disfiguring, (b) black, (c) indelible _____

12. a *disinterested* discussion: (a) boring, (b) impartial, (c) stimulating _____

13. a *strident* voice: (a) low, (b) shrill, (c) stuttering _____

14. devices of *propaganda*: (a) spreading ideas, (b) lies, (c) politics _____

15. the *inherent* supremacy of human beings: (a) intrinsic, (b) unnatural, (c) immoral _____

16. an *anachronism*: (a) severe deformity, (b) event placed in the wrong time, (c) enigma _____

17. *fastidiously* dressed: (a) carefully, (b) prudishly, (c) stylishly _____

18. acting *insouciant*: (a) disrespectful, (b) carefree, (c) impudent _____

19. to *refute* an argument: (a) summarize, (b) disprove, (c) begin _____

20. to treat with *levity*: (a) gaiety, (b) seriousness, (c) haste _____

PARAGRAPHS

Identifying Paragraphs and
Sentence Functions

Paragraphs, like sentences, are distinct units of meaning. Although some paragraphs serve to introduce, to conclude, or to provide transitions, most are used to present and develop ideas. To be effective, each of these paragraphs must possess a single central idea, usually expressed in a **topic sentence**. In most paragraphs, the first sentence is the topic sentence. Notice how the first sentence of the following paragraph controls its direction and development.

> *In panda reproduction the incredible becomes common.* The gestation period is variable, 97 days to 163 days. Most births occur in late August or September. Newborns are about six inches long, and weigh a mere three to four ounces—or 1/900 the weight of the mother; their skin is pink and almost naked, and their eyes are sealed until they are more than a month old. They look like ill-designed rubber toys. Such an underdeveloped infant should need a gestation period of only 45 days. It appears that the panda has delayed implantation, a condition in which the fertilized egg divides a few times to the blastocyst stage and then floats free in the uterus for one and a half to four months before implanting and continuing its growth.
> George B. Schraller. "Secrets of the Wild Panda."
> *National Geographic*. March 1986: 292.

As a general rule, the appearance of a topic sentence signals the beginning of a new paragraph.

Furthermore, every sentence within a paragraph should develop the topic sentence. Sentences that do not clearly support the point of the paragraph but are only vaguely related to its general subject are said to be **digressive**. In the paragraph below, the fourth sentence shifts in focus from the impact of new products on the soft-drink industry to their impact on consumers.

> The soft-drink business is in transition. Recent introductions of non-caffeine colas and of new artificial sweeteners for diet drinks have created new markets. Soft-drink producers who ignore these trends will soon face lower profits. *Some consumers are baffled by the wide range of choices in retail outlets.* Research indicates that these new markets are likely to grow well into the next decade.

Finally, every sentence in a well-focused paragraph must clearly fulfill an identifiable function. In addition to topic sentences, most paragraphs also contain phrases or sentences that help narrow the central idea. These are called **restrictive** elements. Although most paragraphs have a single restriction, more complex ones may have two or more. Most sentences in most paragraphs, though, offer **support** in the form of examples, facts, explanations, definitions, descriptions, or evidence. The sentences in most explanatory paragraphs follow the order of *topic—restriction—support*. In the following paragraphs, topic sentences are introduced with (T), restriction sentences and phrases with (R), and support sentences with (S).

(T) Most farmers don't get subsidies. (R) Participation in the basic crop-subsidy programs is voluntary, and most farmers stay away. (S) A study released in 1984 by the Senate Budget Committee found that the major subsidy programs covered only 21 percent of farms and 16.5 percent of farm acreage.

Gregg Easterbrook.
"Making Sense of Agriculture." *The Atlantic.* July 1985: 63.

(T) Professional boxing is too brutal a sport for any civilized people to tolerate. (R) In the ring, (S) boxers routinely treat spectators to the sight of bruised skin, bloodied noses, torn lips, and swollen eyes. (S) Ray "Boom Boom" Mancini even treated viewers to the death of his opponent. (R) But the damage boxers inflict upon each other is not limited to injuries evident in the ring. (S) Sugar Ray Leonard had his career shortened by a torn retina in his right eye. (S) Muhammad Ali is now suffering from a form of Parkinson's disease caused, many doctors believe, by too many blows to the head.[1]

1. The division of paragraphs into topic, restriction, and illustration slots from A. L. Becker, "A Tagmemic Approach to Paragraph Analysis," reprinted in *The Sentence and the Paragraph* (Urbana, Ill; National Council of Teachers of English, 1966), 33–38.

23.1 Paragraph Division

■ *Divide the following passage into paragraphs by inserting the sign ¶. The original passage contains three paragraphs.*

The Civil War is, for the American imagination, the great single event of our history. Without too much wrenching, it may, in fact, be said to *be* American history. Before the Civil War we had no history in the deepest and most inward sense. There was, of course, the noble vision of the Founding Fathers articulated in the Declaration and the Constitution—the dream of freedom incarnated in a more perfect union. But the Revolution did not create a nation except on paper; and too often in the following years the vision of the Founding Fathers, which men had suffered and died to validate, became merely a daydream of easy and automatic victories, a vulgar delusion of manifest destiny, a conviction of being a people divinely chosen to live on milk and honey at small expense. The vision had not been finally submitted to the test of history. There was little awareness of the cost of having a history. The anguished scrutiny of the meaning of the vision in experience had not become a national reality. It became a reality, and we became a nation, only with the Civil War. The Civil War is our only "felt" history— history lived in the national imagination. This is not to say that the War is always, and by all men, felt in the same way. Quite the contrary. But this fact is an index to the very complexity, depth, and fundamental significance of the event. It is an overwhelming and vital image of human, and national, experience.

Robert Penn Warren. *The Legacy of the Civil War.*
Cambridge: Harvard University Press, 1961, 3–4.

23.2 Paragraph Division

■ *Divide the following passage into paragraphs by inserting the sign ¶. The original passage contains three paragraphs.*

The rationales for saving wild species, at the onset of the movement several decades ago, were largely ethical, esthetic, and ecological. These fundamental arguments have since been joined by another, equally important one. We depend on our fellow species for our material welfare, and ultimately for our future survival, in all sorts of unsuspected ways. Conserving the planet's tropical areas is especially important to realizing the utilitarian benefits of wild species. Some 70 percent of the Earth's plants and animals exist in the tropics, which means—by and large—in developing nations. Third World leaders may be personally aware of the ethical and esthetic values of wildlife, but they also recognize that it is politically unfeasible for their impoverished populations to retain space for rhinos, giraffes, and jaguars when millions of hungry people lack land to grow their crops. If wildlife can "pay its way" in the marketplace and make a local economic contribution, then space may yet be found for threatened species. Although some may view the utilitarian rationale for preserving species as a narrow view of wildlife's true value, there need not be a conflict between the consideration of a species' economic contributions and the belief that its continued existence needs no justification. But faced with expanding human populations, especially in developing nations, we must realize there is less and less room for wildlife that exists for its own sake. We use hundreds of products each day that owe their existence to plants and animals. The ways in which wild species support our daily welfare fall under three main headings: agriculture, medicine, and industry.

Norman Myers.
"By Saving Wild Species, We May Be Saving Ourselves."

1. _____

   _____

2. _____

   _____

3. _____

   _____

4. _____

   _____

23.3 Paragraph Division

■ *Divide the following passage into paragraphs by inserting the sign ¶. The original passage contains four paragraphs.*

The crucial role of journalism in a democracy is to provide a common ground of knowledge and analysis, a meeting place for national debate: it is the link between people and institutions. Without the information provided by newspapers and TV, citizens would have little basis for deciding what to believe and whom to support. Just as a pervasive mistrust of police could cause a breakdown of order, a growing hostility to the press could sever the ligaments of a workable society. Moreover, without a strong and trusted press, people would have almost no way to keep their government and other big institutions honest. Government, particularly the federal Establishment, has vast powers to mislead the people and manage the news. Officials can conceal impending actions until their effects are irreversible. Other big institutions—corporations, unions, hospitals, police forces—prefer to cloak their decision-making process and their performance from the scrutiny of the public, whose lives may be deeply affected. And despite the passage of shield laws to protect journalists from having to reveal sources, they are regularly subpoenaed to testify about what they have reported. Journalists became so aggressive partly because they knew, contrary to the widely held public view, that they were Davids fighting Goliaths. As the press itself grows into a more powerful institution, it must be careful how it uses its strength, whether it faces an ordinary individual or a president: the attempt to uncover can too easily turn into the impulse to tear apart. Freedom of the press, like any other freedom, can be dangerous. But Thomas Jefferson, who suffered at the hands of journalists as much as any contemporary politician, insisted that protecting the press at its worst was an essential part of having the press be free.

William A. Henry III.
"Journalism Under Fire."

23.4 Digressive Sentences

■ *In the blank at the bottom of each paragraph, write the number of any sentence that is digressive. In any paragraph there may be as many as three such sentences.*

EXAMPLE

(1) To use a library efficiently one must first learn how books are classified in the computerized catalog. (2) These catalogs are located usually on a library's main floor—but not always. (3) Books are listed in three ways: by author, by title, and by subject. (4) Thus if one knows a title, but not an author or a subject, one can easily locate a book.

A. (1) One of the most overused words today is "major." (2) This is not the army or marine rank. (3) No company would dare list a new program as a "minor" one. (4) And what politician would ever deliver a "short talk"? (5) Any speech no matter how insignificant must be labeled a "major address to the American people." (6) Thus "major" takes its place alongside "startling new discovery" and the many other expressions that have undermined our language.

_____

B. (1) Financial aid for students includes basic grants, work-study jobs, scholarships, and loans. (2) In the past, students who required financial assistance often had to drop out of school and work for a few months. (3) Many students simultaneously receive aid from several of these sources, usually combining scholarships with work-study programs. (4) College administrations continually solicit alumni for more money. (5) Jobs are especially popular because they may provide valuable experience for a future vocation. (6) Some of the country's most distinguished citizens received scholarships. (7) All students in need of financial assistance qualify for aid in one form or another. (8) Even if they must borrow from university loan funds, they usually pay only minimal interest charges. (9) Students who desire assistance should contact their school's financial aid office for further information.

_____

C.   (1) Almost any backyard can be transformed into a showcase wildlife habitat. (2) Birdfeeders, birdbaths, small fishponds—all combined with the right shrubs and trees—will attract a variety of wildlife. (3) Many neighbors may want to transform their yards as well. (4) Now several species of wildlife are steadily losing their natural habitat to industry and agriculture. (5) Shrubs (such as hawthorne, crab apple, and silky dogwood) and hardwood trees (like oak or beech) serve small animals and many songbirds. (6) In addition, colorful annual flowers attract many helpful insects. (7) If enough fresh water is available, ducks, raccoons, frogs, and crayfish will soon visit. (8) Backyard ecology is especially popular among youth.

D.   (1) To see the Grand Canyon as it should be seen, a visitor must rise before dawn. (2) The canyon is located in northern Arizona. (3) Just before the sun appears the walls of the canyon are a deep purple, and a visitor almost feels the eerie silence. (4) Gradually the canyon comes alive. (5) Soon there are the cries of a few birds. (6) Then with the first streaks of light, the rocks begin to glow in rich oranges and reds. (7) Finally, the details appear—the deep crevices, the patches of grass and mesquite and sage—and a visitor who looks closely may see a deer or chipmunk. (8) Later the visitor can visit the many shops located near Bright Angel Lodge and El Tovar.

E.   (1) The great cities before Rome (Corinth, Carthage, Syracuse) were trading and manufacturing centers. (2) Rome, on the other hand, was the financial and political capital of the Western world. (3) Rome never rivaled previous great cities in commerce or industry. (4) Another great city of the ancient world was Carthage, located in North Africa. (5) Rome usually imported most of its necessities and luxuries from cities and regions under its military and political control. (6) Sicily and Africa especially provided for Rome's agricultural needs such as corn. (7) During the so-called Golden Age of Greece, Athens was the intellectual center of Western civilization.

F.   (1) What does television mean to the American family? (2) Many people enjoy adventure shows, comedies, and detective shows. (3) Ask those who work at home what they enjoy on television and learn the sordid details in the lives of every character on "As the World Turns" and "All My Children." (4) Ask any husband which comes first, the news or dinner, and hear how important it is to keep informed by watching Dan Rather report from Washington. (5) And how many of us have heard some child wail, "I don't have anything to do!" when the TV is at the shop? (6) One can only

346

wonder if our founding fathers ever could have envisioned television as our principal means to achieve "life, liberty, and the pursuit of happiness."

G.   (1) The modern photographer needs more than a simple developing kit to process photographs at home. (2) Actually, developing them at home is probably more expensive than sending them to professional laboratories to develop them. (3) The most important and most expensive item required for film processing is a good enlarger. (4) If one develops negatives without an enlarger, then the final pictures are almost too small to enjoy. (5) Used enlargers for sale are very difficult to find. (6) Furthermore, one should purchase an enlarging easel, an enlarger timer, and a focusing lens. (7) Only after buying this relatively expensive equipment can the amateur photographer hope to develop good-quality prints.

H.   (1) Many expressions have been used to describe the second half of the twentieth century. (2) With enormous arrogance we have called our brief period of history the nuclear age or the age of progress and cavalierly ignored any improvements in the human lot that were produced over the last several thousand years. (3) Perhaps we should reassess our view of ourselves and look a bit to the world we inherited. (4) Moreover, we have created more waste, expended more of the earth's natural resources, spent more money and time on frivolities and entertainment, and, as far as we can see into the future at this moment, left generations to come with greater problems to solve than any previous generation left to its successors in the entire span of human history. (5) We have proclaimed this the era of progress, but future generations may one day mock us for our vanity. (6) We should all try to improve our environment.

I.   (1) Archaeology is a much more exact science than many people realize. (2) For example, archaeologists have determined that, on a day in late spring approximately 400,000 years ago, about twenty-five people made a brief visit to a cove on the Mediterranean coast near Nice, France. (3) From the study of fossil bones, stone tools, various imprints in the sand, and the density of the sand, scientists have reconstructed in detail much of the three-day sojourn. (4) Imprints give clues to where these ancient people slept and what they slept on. (5) Archaeology has really matured as a science and has become quite popular in the public's eye since Heinrich Schliemann's excavation of ancient cities in the late nineteenth century. (6) These imaginative scientists also know much about the food these nomadic people ate, how they prepared it, how they hunted for food, and how they protected the group from predators at night. (7) The human imagination simply has no limits.

J.   (1) When people complain about the outlandish fashions of the great contemporary American and French designers, someone should remind them that this is not the only age to flaunt the outrageous in wearing apparel. (2) These clothes may be purchased at most major department stores and in many boutiques across the country. (3) For sheer absurdity we have to look only to the zoot suit of the 1940s, or, if we are truly interested in the bizarre, we might remember the bustle and bloomers. (4) No age has been without its oddities. (5) We can only be thankful that so few of them became permanent additions to our wardrobes.

K.   (1) Public meetings between management and labor can be beneficial. (2) But one should not expect miracles. (3) Formal negotiations also may be detrimental if either side plays only to the press. (4) Informal contacts usually precede public meetings and set agendas. (5) This procedure often reduces the possibility of either side grandstanding for publicity. (6) Indeed, these contacts usually are necessary for productive bargaining.

L.   (1) Successful interviewing for a job requires careful planning. (2) Some study of the prospective employer is necessary. (3) Factual knowledge about a firm or industry impresses personnel managers. (4) One should research the company or firm thoroughly in a library or through personal contacts with other employees. (5) The successful candidate knows the company's goals and makes them his or her own.

M.   (1) Changing patterns of weather may cause dramatic shifts in population. (2) When climates change, land that once was fertile may become desert. (3) People must move, or many face starvation if they live in areas where irrigation is not possible. (4) Weather and population are inextricably linked. (5) Crops and livestock must have adequate rainfall.

N.　　(1) The American bald eagle seems to be making a comeback. (2) Once on the verge of extinction, the eagle now has increased its population throughout most of its range. (3) DDT pollution caused severe problems for the bald eagle. (4) It is now protected by law against hunters. (5) If not healthy, the bald eagle population has at least increased significantly.

———————————

23.5 Sentence Functions

■ *Label the sentences in the following paragraph. Use **T** to identify the topic sentence, **R** to identify the restricting sentence(s), and **S** to identify supporting sentences.*

_____ It's not just in behavioral laboratories that animals display their cognitive powers, but also in the wild. _____ In fact, field biologists are finding that many species' natural behaviors are no less complex than the ones that psychologists are going to such lengths to teach them. _____ Research has shown, for example, that the calls of some free-ranging monkeys are not just raw expressions of arousal, as was long assumed, but fairly detailed news reports about events in the outside world. _____ Robert Syfarth and Dorothy Cheney of the University of Pennsylvania have found that vervet monkeys in Kenya have at least three distinct alarm calls—one for snakes, one for eagles, one for leopards—and that each one elicits a different response.

Geoffrey Cowley. "The Wisdom of Animals."
Newsweek. 28 May 1988: 56–57.

NAME _____

DATE _____ SCORE _____

23.6 Sentence Functions

■ *Label the sentences in the following paragraph. Use **T** to identify the topic sentence, **R** to identify the restricting sentence(s), and **S** to identify supporting sentences.*

_____ It was on the silver screen that the soda fountain truly reached stardom. _____ From the 1920s through the early '50s, the drugstore set was a Hollywood fixture. _____ D. W. Griffith was one of the first to explore the fountain's possibilities; in his 1919 charmer, *True Heart Suzie,* Lillian Gish is courted there weekly. _____ W. C. Fields' *It's the Old Army Game* (1926) is facetiously dedicated to the American druggist. _____ It was beside the fountain in 1938 that Mickey Rooney, as the quintessential teenager Andy Hardy, flirted with Judy Garland in *Love Finds Andy Hardy.* _____ With the box-office success of the Hardy series, the list of fountain-featuring films grew at a phenomenal pace.

David M. Schwartz. "Life Was Sweeter, and More Innocent, in Our Soda Days."
Smithsonian. July 1986: 116.

23.7 Sentence Functions

■ *Label the sentences in the following paragraph. Use **T** to identify the topic sentence, **R** to identify the restricting sentence(s), and **S** to identify supporting sentences.*

_____ Mindful of . . . problems and of costs, solar designers have been moving away from active systems and toward passive techniques, such as concentrating the house's windows on the south side and installing a six-inch-thick masonry floor, topped with tile or brick, to absorb sunshine and gradually release heat hours later. _____ Passive solar devices are becoming increasingly sophisticated. _____ Trombe walls—thick masonry walls recessed a few inches from an exterior wall of glass—were briefly popular among solar designers, but they interfered too much with views to attract a wide market. _____ Big plastic tubes filled with water to absorb heat have encountered similar resistance because of their obtrusiveness. _____ The favored instruments of solar today demand no aesthetic sacrifice; some even add to the pleasure of the environment. _____ One common device is a fireplace with an enlarged chimney wall situated so that it catches the sun several hours a day.

Philip Langdon. "The American House."
The Atlantic. September 1984: 55.

Paragraph Development

The kind of support offered in a paragraph, as well as the order in which it is presented, depends on the paragraph's purpose. Most paragraphs fall into one of the categories listed below.

OPENING AND CLOSING PARAGRAPHS

An opening paragraph can have several functions. First, it must present enough background explanation to help the reader see the context, the relevance, and the importance of the discussion. The paragraph might also entice its reader to continue reading by presenting an eye-catching fact, description, example, or assertion. Finally, it must present the main idea or thesis and thus orient the reader to the discussion that follows. In opening paragraphs, the background and interest-creating material generally precede the thesis statement. Notice how the following paragraph introduces a discussion of a new trend in aircraft design.

> With their swept-back wings, forward-mounted canards, or stabilizers, and pusher propellers, they look a little as if they should be moving through the air tailfirst. But the two new designs—Beech Aircraft's Starship and Rinaldo Piaggio's P. 180 Avanti—are very much forward-looking pieces of machinery. Using advanced technology to deliver high performance and good fuel efficiency, they could dictate the shape of small transport aircraft in the coming years.
> Philip Elmer-Dewitt. "The Shape of Planes to Come." *Time* 27 June 1988: 65.

Closing paragraphs also have several functions. They may reassert the general relevance of the discussion, explore its ramifications, or concede its limitations. If the discussion has been long or complicated, the closing paragraph may reiterate the essay's major points. Elmer-Dewitt closes his article on new airplane designs by recognizing potential marketing difficulties. He quotes Henry Ogrodzinski, the communications director of the General Aviation Manufacturers Association, whom he had introduced in an earlier paragraph.

> How much the demand will benefit the Starship and the Avanti is uncertain. The manufacturers still have to demonstrate that their performance claims are valid. Moreover, some executives may not like the idea of entrusting their lives to such novel and unusual designs. Ogrodzinski, for one, thinks they will. "Looks and status have always been a selling point in corporate aircraft," he says. "There is a certain prestige in owning the latest design."

PARAGRAPHS OF DESCRIPTION

Descriptive paragraphs help the reader envision a person or group of people, a place, an object, or an event. These paragraphs are usually developed by details that answer such common questions as who, what, when, where, why, and how about the subject. At other times they are developed by details that appeal to the reader's senses of hearing, sight, touch, even smell and taste. The details in these paragraphs are usually organized by time or place. Garrison Keillor's description below, for example, is organized by place, moving from near to far as he first describes a house, then the barnyard behind it, then the fields beyond.

> In 1970, . . . I moved out to a farmhouse on the rolling prairie in central Minnesota, near Freeport, where I planted a garden and wrote stories to support my wife and year-old son. Rent was $80 a month. It got us a big square brick house with a porch that looked out on a peaceful barnyard, a granary and machine sheds and corncribs and silo, and the barn and feedlot where Norbert, the farmer whom I rented from, kept his beef cattle. Beyond the windbreak of red oak and spruce to the west and north lay a hundred sixty acres of his corn and oats. . . . Our long two-rut driveway ran due north through the woods to where the gravel road made an L, where our mailbox stood, where you could stand and see for a couple miles in all directions. . . .
>
> Garrison Keillor. "Laying on Our Backs Looking Up at the Stars."
> *Newsweek.* 4 July 1988: 32.

PARAGRAPHS OF DEFINITION

Whereas descriptive paragraphs help readers understand concrete subjects, paragraphs of definition help them understand abstract ones. Usually they clarify the meaning of ideas, special, unusual, or technical terms, or even proposals. These paragraphs typically begin by identifying and describing their subject's distinguishing characteristics and by presenting examples. To convey a clear, complete, and balanced impression, a defining paragraph might also include points about what the subject is *not*.

> To my biased taste, Cantonese cuisine is the greatest of all the Chinese cookery. The classical Cantonese style emphasizes freshness of ingredients and subtle but distinct contrasts of tastes and textures. A single dish is often composed of sweet and sour flavors, crispy and creamy or crunchy and tender textures and hot and cold temperatures. Gentle, quick cooking preserves the delicate natural flavors, colors and aromas of this fresh food. Soy, hoisin and oyster sauces—all relatively mild and congenial—are its mainstays. There is not overdose of garlic, sharp spices and heavy oils. It is definitely not greasy.
>
> Ken Hom. "The Road to Canton." *The New York Times Magazine.* 5 June 1988: 57.

In this paragraph, Ken Hom defines Cantonese cuisine by describing first its general characteristics then by identifying its typical ingredients.

As the paragraph concludes, he distinguishes its flavors from those characteristic of other types of food.

PARAGRAPHS OF COMPARISON AND CONTRAST

Paragraphs may offer literal comparisons of persons, places, proposals, objects, or ideas, or they may offer figurative comparisons, called **analogies**. Paragraphs may also identify the differences between two things that appear similar. Such paragraphs of comparison and contrast usually identify specific points of similarity or dissimilarity between the two things being compared. Any of the points used to describe or define may be used as features to compare or contrast. The following paragraph, for example, contrasts the positive and negative factors affecting the marketability of commercially-raised venison in New Zealand.

> Deer have some advantages over cattle and sheep as food. Venison is lean, about 10 percent fat compared to more than 20 percent for lamb or beef. Thus it appeals to today's calorie-conscious markets. It is, however, more expensive—farm prices are almost $6 per kilogram in New Zealand compared to $1.60 for beef or $.70 for lamb.
>
> T. H. Clutton-Brock. "Red Deer and Man." *National Geographic*. October 1986: 550.

PARAGRAPHS OF ANALYSIS

Analytical paragraphs divide a large group of ideas, events, objects, or people into parts. They can take several forms.

Paragraphs that analyze through **classification and division** show the way in which a single item or a group of items can be logically divided into discrete parts. In these paragraphs, each subcategory is briefly defined, and the subcategories may be compared or contrasted with each other. In the following paragraph, Thomas Pyles classifies American regional dialects by the places they occur.

> In American English there are three main regional types—Northern, Midland, and Southern—with a good many different blendings of these as one travels westward. . . . There are also a number of subtypes on the Atlantic Coast, such as the speech of the New York and Boston areas in the North and the Charleston-Savannah area in the South. All types of American English have grown out of the regional modifications of the British Standard—with some coloring from the British dialects—as it existed in the seventeenth century, when it was much less rigid than it is today.
>
> Thomas Pyles. *The Origins and Development of the English Language*. 2nd. ed. New York: Harcourt, 1971, 235.

Paragraphs that analyze **cause and effect** show how past events or situations affect events or situations that follow them or how present situations or events may affect the future. These paragraphs list several causes or effects or explain a single one. The following paragraph presents some projected long term effects from a change in the earth's atmosphere.

With a diminished ozone layer, more UV [ultraviolet radiation] from the sun will reach the earth. Scientists believe that more UV will induce mutations in the organisms that anchor the food chain of the world's oceans. UV threatens not only to cause more cases of skin cancer but also to damage the immune system, a blow that could leave us defenseless against infectious diseases. More UV may damage crops worth billions of dollars. "It is no exaggeration to say that the health and safety of millions of people around the world are at stake," says David Doniger of the Natural Resources Defense Council.

Sharon Begley. "A Gaping Hole in the Sky." *Newsweek.* 11 July 1988: 21.

Paragraphs that analyze **process** divide an action into a series of steps. These paragraphs identify, then describe or define, each step involved. They are always arranged from first to last in strictly chronological order. Notice how the following paragraph specifies the steps involved in successfully planting one species of grape.

For a maximum fruit production, use a wire trellis; it provides the best support for muscadines. To build a trellis, first drive a 4- to 5-foot stake into the ground beside the vine at planting time. Then, when the vine starts growing, select the strongest shoot to become the main stem and tie it to the stake. During the first summer, remove all side shoots. When the stem reaches the top of the stake, pinch off its tip to encourage growth of side shoots.

Steve Bender. "The Not-So-Lowly Muscadine." *Progressive Farmer*. July 1988: 59.

PARAGRAPHS OF ASSERTION

Perhaps the most common type of paragraph supports a statement of belief, an assertion of value, a judgment, or a generalization. These paragraphs are usually supported by facts, examples, statistics, statements by authorities, or eyewitness accounts. The paragraph below uses historical facts to support its assertion about Olympic Games of the past.

In fact, the Games of the Greeks were just as flawed as our own. It was the Greek tyrant Pheidon of Argos who seized Olympia in the seventh century B.C. for the glorification of his strong-arm regime. Two neighboring city-states, Elis and Pisa, fought for generations over the right to control the Games and collect their revenues. Sometimes such conflicts ended in an "An-Olympiad" or non-Olympics: the Games did not always go on.

Frank Holt. "An Olympic-Size Delusion." *Newsweek*. 16 July 1984: 16.

24.1 Paragraph Development

■ *Identify the type of development (description, definition, comparison and contrast, classification/division analysis, cause and effect analysis, process analysis, or assertion with support) used in each of the following paragraphs.*

1.   Even the kindest and most well-intentioned parent will sometimes become exasperated. The difference between the good and the not-so-good parent in such situations is that the good parent will realize that his exasperation probably has more to do with himself than with what the child did, and that showing his exasperation will not be to anyone's advantage. The not-so-good parent, in contrast, believes that his exasperation was caused only by his child and that therefore he has every right to act on it.

> Bruno Bettelheim. "Punishment versus Discipline."
> *The Atlantic*. November 1985: 52.

Method of development: _____

2.   Most women don't have the luxury of choice. They work because they have to. The majority of mothers with children under eighteen today are in the labor force—including nearly half of all married women with children under the age of one—and the majority of them, 71 percent, have full-time jobs. Because of the high divorce rate and an increase in the number of single mothers, one-fifth of all families with children are now headed by women. Other factors push married women into the work force. It now takes two wage earners to sustain the same middle-class lifestyle that one income could provide twenty years ago.

> Barbara Kantrowitz. "A Mother's Choice." *Newsweek* 31 March 1986: 47.

Method of development: _____

3.   The male eagle is a model husband for these times. He does his share of home building by gathering sticks—often six feet long—for the base of the nest. Barreling into the desired branch at full speed, he hits it with his feet, grabs it with his talons as it cracks and flies away with it. He takes his turn sitting on the nest and helps feed and care for the newborns. According to Hodges's current study, one of the parents remains at the nest constantly until the eaglets are four weeks old.

> Sharon Begley. "Comeback for a National Symbol." *Newsweek*. 9 July 1984: 65.

Method of development: _____

4.   Amid five acres of paddocks, pens, and fields stands a sturdy roundhouse, more than forty feet in diameter and thirty feet high, its basketwork walls plastered with daub. The thatched, conical roof, where swallows nest, protects ovens and querns and crockery. Immediately outside are several haystacks and a byre. A low bank and a shallow dike enclose the central compound. Beyond lie fields of wheat, barley, beans, and flax. In outlying pastures livestock graze—unusual breeds of sheep and cattle, gamey and hirsute.

Cullen Murphy. "The Buster Experiment."
The Atlantic. August 1985: 20.

Method of development: _____

24.2 Paragraph Development

■ *Identify the type of development (description, definition, comparison and contrast, classification/division analysis, cause and effect analysis, process analysis, or assertion with support) used in each of the following paragraphs.*

1.　　One good way to knead is to push hard into the dough with both heels of your hands and then pull the top edge toward you, so that it looks like the crest of a wave. When the dough is too stiff to be stirred, it's ready to be kneaded. Cover a flat surface and your hands with flour, keeping track of how much you use by taking it from the remaining cup or so. Knead more flour in by tablespoons, adding it as the white powder disappears.

> Corby Kummer. "Parlor Pizza."
> *The Atlantic.* April 1985: 129.

Method of development: _____

2.　　As for meat, 43 game species relied on by various hunter and gatherer groups averaged only 4.3 percent fats, compared to 25 to 35 percent in supermarket meat. The fat of game meat also tends to be much less saturated, meaning less harmful. Overall, the average diet of hunters and gatherers consisted of 33 percent protein, compared to 12 percent in the modern American diet; an equal percentage (46) of carbohydrates, and 21 percent fat (with a high ratio of polyunsaturates), compared to our 42 percent. Hunter-gatherer sodium consumption is estimated at 690 milligrams daily, as compared to between 2,000 and 7,000 for present-day Americans.

> Melvin Konnor. "What Our Ancestors Ate." *New York Times Magazine.* 5 June
> 1988: 54–55.

Method of development: _____

3.　　I see several advantages to reintegrating grammar into the writing curriculum under this new conception of its role. First, teachers have an incentive to teach it more frequently and with more enthusiasm. Second, the public can take heart that we are getting "back to basics" at last. As always, of course, some people will not learn even the handbook rules; some will learn those and nothing more; and some will find the handbook rules a help in learning the real grammar of the written language. Perhaps more students will learn to write grammatical prose, but that is less important than that more students may discover what it means to write well.

Geoffrey Nunberg. "An Apology for Grammar."
National Forum. Fall 1985: 15.

Method of development: _____

4.   A public philosophy gives meaning and coherence to what would otherwise seem random phenomena: a starving child, a shuttered factory, a new Russian missile. By "public philosophy" I mean something less rigid and encompassing than an ideology but also less ephemeral than the "public mood." I have in mind a set of assumptions and logical links by which we interpret and integrate social reality. A public philosophy informs our senses of what our society is about, what it is *for*.

Robert Reich. "Toward a New Public Philosophy."
The Atlantic. May 1985: 68.

Method of development: _____

Paragraph Transitions

Paragraphs are easier for readers to follow when the connections between the various words, sentences, and ideas are easy to detect. To clarify these connections, place every sentence in a clear relationship with every other sentence in the paragraph, and effectively use an array of transitional devices.

SENTENCE RELATIONSHIPS

A sentence can be either **coordinate** with or **subordinate** to the preceding sentence. If coordinate, it will offer a parallel idea and perhaps additional examples or detail. If subordinate, it will describe, restrict, explain, or qualify the preceding sentence.

Sentences in the paragraph below are numbered and indented to show their relative relationships. Every sentence is modified and explained by the sentences with higher numbers that follow. Sentences with the same number are coordinate and equally modify or develop preceding sentences.

1. Juvenile delinquents do not have to go to prison to be reformed.
  2. All over the world, programs have been created to help these teenage offenders.
    3. In India, there are penal educational institutions for juveniles.
    3. In Cuba, youth organizations are being formed to provide activities and educational programs in child-rearing.
      4. There, the Ministry of Education holds meetings with parents about child-rearing and discipline.
      4. It also sends tempted youth to a school where crime opportunities are reduced.
      4. If Cuban youngsters are convicted of a crime, they are sent to labor camps or to isolated training schools.
      4. The offenders may also be sent to an agricultural school, where they can do some constructive work.[2]

The first sentence identifies the topic of the paragraph: juvenile delinquents can be reformed without being sent to prison. The second sentence further restricts the topic by suggesting that alternatives can be found in other nations. Sentences three and four offer support by providing examples of such alternatives. Sentences five through eight all further describe the alternatives used in one of those nations.

2. Identification of the function of different levels of generality within paragraphs from Francis Christensen, "A Generative Rhetoric of the Paragraph" in *Notes Toward a New Rhetoric: Six Essays for Teachers* (New York: Harper, 1967: 52–81).

TRANSITIONAL DEVICES

Effective writers use various elements of style to help clarify and explain the relationships between sentences. Transitional words and phrases, reference words, repeated words, and repeated sentence patterns are all ways to show these relationships.

Transitional words and phrases can indicate time and place (*before, while, during, when, where*), addition (*and, furthermore, in fact*), contrast (*but, however, although, on the other hand*), or causation (*so, therefore, consequently, because*).

Reference words include personal pronouns (*her, he, hers, his, its, their, they*), demonstrative adjectives (*this, those, these, that*), and comparatives (*more, less, greater, fewer*).

Repeated words include not only the same words but also synonyms and general terms of class that include words used earlier. In the following sentence, *students* is a class term referring back to the more specific word *freshmen*.

> Many freshmen find registration bewildering. These students quickly learn ways to make the process more tolerable.

In the following passage, transitional words and phrases are underlined once, reference words are underlined twice, and repeated words or variations on the same word are circled.

> Throughout, the original intention of scholarship persists, whether duly or poorly carried out: it is analysis—that is, the narrow scrutiny of an object for the purpose of drawing conclusions. These in turn must be supported by original arguments and must take into account the previous arguments of others, known as "the literature" of the subject. It is clear that as the analysts multiply and the literature accumulates, the subject that anyone is able to deal with grows smaller. In other words, specialization is unavoidable; and thus it is that specialism, which is a state of mind, follows specialization, which is a practical necessity.

Jacques Barzun. "Scholarship Versus Culture." *The Atlantic.* November 1984: 99.

Repeated sentence structure helps to clarify sentence relationships. Often sentences that present parallel reasons or explanations do so in grammatically parallel ways. Sentences at different levels of specificity should not be grammatically parallel, however. Notice how repeated structure helps tie together the sentences in the following paragraph.

Yet punctuation is something more than a culture's birthmark; it scores the music in our minds, gets our thoughts moving to the rhythm of our hearts. Punctuation is the notation in the sheet music of our words, telling us when to rest, or when to raise our voices; it acknowledges that the meaning of our discourse, as of any symphonic composition, lies not in the units but in the pauses, the pacing and the phrasing. Punctuation is the way one bats one's eyes, lowers one's voice, or blushes demurely. Punctuation adjusts the tone and color and volume till the feeling comes into perfect focus.

Pico Iyer. "In Praise of the Humble Comma." *Time*. 13 June 1988: 80.

25.1 Sentence Relationships

■ *Place numbers in the blanks before each sentence to illustrate the coordinate and subordinate relationships of the sentences within the paragraph. Label the most general sentence (the topic sentence)* **1**. *Use higher numbers for the sentences that follow. Sentences that are coordinate should have the same number. Sentences that are subordinate should have higher numbers than the sentences they help explain.*

_____ "People research," or "psychographics," as this kind of market research is known, has been around for a while. _____ The Yankelovich Monitor, devised by Daniel Yankelovich, began measuring the effects of social trends on consumers in the early seventies, and a number of advertising firms have done elaborate surveys classifying consumers into categories and psychological types. _____ In 1970 Benton & Bowles interviewed 2,000 housewives and came up with six categories (Outgoing Optimists, Conscientious Vigilants, and so on); _____ in 1975 Needham, Harper & Steers identified five male and five female prototypes, among them the Self-Made Businessman, the Frustrated Factory-Worker, and the Militant Mother.

James Atlas. "Beyond Demographics."
The Atlantic. October 1984: 50–51.

25.2 Sentence Relationships

■ *Place numbers in the blanks before each sentence to illustrate the coordinate and subordinate relationships of the sentences within the paragraph. Label the most general sentence (the topic sentence) 1. Use higher numbers for the sentences that follow. Sentences that are coordinate should have the same number. Sentences that are subordinate should have higher numbers than the sentences they help explain.*

_____ To fully appreciate the technology's revolutionary impact, however, you've got to get out of the house. _____ These days video permeates virtually every corner of our culture, inexorably and irrevocably transforming the mechanisms by which millions of us define who and what we are. _____ Just look around. _____ It's in classrooms, courtrooms, board rooms, and operating rooms. _____ It's on the floor of Congress and above the supermarket checkout line. It looms large on stadium scoreboards and hangs from the ceiling in fashion emporiums. _____ It has swallowed the music industry and, in the process, gotten the generations at it again, this time over the sex-and-violence content of MTV rock videos aimed at the young.

Harry F. Waters. "The Age of Video."
Newsweek. 30 December 1988: 45.

NAME _____

DATE _____ SCORE _____

25.3 Sentence Relationships

■ *Place numbers in the blanks before each sentence to illustrate the coordinate and subordinate relationships of the sentences within the paragraph. Label the most general sentence (the topic sentence) **1**. Use higher numbers for the sentences that follow. Sentences that are coordinate should have the same number. Sentences that are subordinate should have higher numbers than the sentences they help explain.*

_____ To the creator of the first intelligence test, the French psychologist Alfred Binet, *IQ* meant something very different from what it has come to imply. _____ As has often been told, Binet was commissioned by the French Ministry of Instruction of develop a test to identify children in need of remedial schooling. _____ He came up with a list of simple tasks that would illustrate the child's "mental age"—a normal three-year-old should be able to point to his nose, eyes, and mouth, a normal ten-year-old should be able to make a sentence with the words *Paris, fortune,* and *gutter,* and so forth. _____ The ratio between mental age and chronological age, of course, yielded the "intelligence quotient," or *IQ,* with 100 defined as normal.

James Fallows. "The Case Against Credentialism."
The Atlantic. December 1985: 55.

25.4 Transitions

■ *Underline once the transitional words and phrases. Underline twice the reference words, including pronouns, demonstrative adjectives, and comparative words. Circle the repeated words, including same words as well as synonyms and terms of class.*

All moose are of a single circumpolar species, *Alces alces*, found in most of Canada, northern Russia, a corner of Poland and parts of Scandinavia, as well as Alaska and the previously mentioned states. In Sweden, moose are so plentiful in some areas that they pose a serious traffic hazard. The same is true in parts of Alaska. On the Kenai Peninsula, as many as 250 moose have been killed on the highways in one year. But although a one-ton car can readily triumph over a half-ton moose, it's a Pyrrhic victory. As one Alaskan wildlife biologist puts it: "You've seen the damage an ordinary white-tailed deer can do to a car? You should see what a bull moose can do!"

John Madson. "The North Woods: A Horn of Plenty for Old Bucketnose."
Smithsonian. July 1986: 104.

25.5 Transitions

◼ *Underline once the transitional words and phrases. Underline twice the reference words, including pronouns, demonstrative adjectives, and comparative words. Circle the repeated words, including same words as well as synonyms and terms of class.*

Chaplin's impact was so strong and swift that within months of his screen debut he was one of the movies' biggest stars. By the end of the first year in films he was, without exaggeration, the most famous man in the world. It didn't take a high-priced media campaign to orchestrate his success; the public made him a star. It was said that all a theater manager had to do to guarantee a crowd was to place in front of his box office a cardboard cutout of the Tramp bearing the slogan "He's Here Today!" He inspired toys, dolls, comic strips, popular songs, highbrow articles, lowbrow imitators, and unprecedented adulation— all of this before TV or radio to help spread the word. Even today, a major computer company, IBM, has chosen the Tramp to represent Everyman who struggles to survive in the high-tech '80's.

Leonard Matlin. "Silent-Film Buffs Stalk and Find a Missing Tramp." *Smithsonian.*
July 1986: 46–47.

Cross-References to
PRACTICAL ENGLISH HANDBOOK, *Eighth Edition*